DCPL000

KV-575-086

WITHDRAWN FROM STOCK
DUBLIN CITY PUBLIC LIBRARIES

Brainse Bhaile Thormod   Tel. 6269324/5
Ballyfermot Library

THE INFORMER

Tom Murphy

Also by Tom Murphy

A Whistle in the Dark

On the Outside (w. Noel O'Donoghue)

On the Inside

A Crucial Week in the Life of a Grocer's Assistant

Famine

The Morning after Optimism

The Sanctuary Lamp

The Blue Macushla

The Informer (from the novel by Liam O'Flaherty)

Conversations on a Homecoming

Bailegangaire

A Thief of a Christmas

Too Late for Logic

The Patriot Game

She Stoops to Folly (from *The Vicar of Wakefield* by Oliver Goldsmith)

The Gigli Concert

The Wake

The House

The Cherry Orchard (a version)

Alice Trilogy

THE INFORMER

Adapted from the novel by Liam O'Flaherty

by Tom Murphy

A Carysfort Press Book

The Informer
Adapted from the novel by Liam O'Flaherty
by Tom Murphy

First published as a paperback in Ireland in 2008
by Carysfort Press Ltd
58 Woodfield, Scholarstown Road, Dublin 16, Ireland

ISBN 978-1-904505-37-2
© 2008 Copyright remains with the author
Printed and bound by eprint limited
Unit 35, Coolmine Industrial Estate, Dublin 15, Ireland

Cover design by Margaret Hamilton
Typeset by Carysfort Press Ltd

This book is published with the financial assistance of The Arts
Council (An Chomhairle Ealaíon), Dublin, Ireland, under the
Title by Title Scheme

Performing Rights. All professional and performing rights are strictly reserved.
Application for permission for performance should be made before rehearsals begin to:
Alexandra Cann Representation, 12, Abingdon Road, London W8 6AF

Caution: All rights reserved. No part of this book may be printed or reproduced
or utilized in any form or by any electronic, mechanical, or other means, now known
or hereafter invented including photocopying and recording, or in any information
storage or retrieval system without permission in writing from the publishers.

This book is sold subject to the conditions that it shall not, by way of trade or otherwise,
be lent, resold, hired out, or otherwise circulated in any form of binding, or cover other
than that in which it is published and without a similar condition, including this
condition, being imposed on the subsequent purchaser.

for Noel Pearson

Tom Murphy's adaptation of *The Informer* was first presented by Noel Pearson at the Olympia Theatre, Dublin, on 13 October 1981, as part of the Dublin Theatre Festival.

The cast was as follows:

Gypo Nolan	Liam Neeson
Gallagher	Alan Barry
Mary McPhilip	Ruth Hegarty
Katie Fox	Barbara Brennan
Louisa Cummins	Aine Ní Mhuiri
Frankie McPhilip	Jim Caffrey
Father (Jack McPhilip)	Gerry Sullivan
Aunt Betty	Marie Kean
Maggie Clancy	Marie Conmee

Other parts were played by: Paul Conway, Don Foley, Phyl Horgan, Maura Keeley, Tom Laidlaw, Pat Layde, Finton McKeown, Fidelma O'Dowda, Charles Roberts, Bernice Toolan

Director	Tom Murphy
Set Designer	Wendy Shea
Costume Designer	Joan Bergin
Lighting Designer	Rupert Murray

Characters

Gypo

Gallagher

Katie Fox

Louisa Cummins

Mary McPhilip

Frankie McPhilip

Father (Jack McPhilip)

Maggie Clancy

Aunt Betty

Mulligan

Mulholland

Connors

Neighbours, Loiterers, Judges, Guards, Whores...

Dublin, 1920s

(Note: This 2008 script is a rewrite of the 1981 adaptation.)

SCENE ONE

*A room in a basement, an oil lamp throwing shadows. Three hooded figures, **JUDGES**, in overcoats, sit behind a table. A man in a shirt and trousers, seated: **MULLIGAN**, asthmatic, emaciated, is crying to himself. There are, say, three **GUARDS**: one standing behind Mulligan, one at the steps that lead up and out of the basement and one on the top step, going in and out of the entrance.*

*And there's **GALLAGHER**, 30–40, a long overcoat that stretches from his neck to his ankles. (There's a sadistic streak in him.) And **MARY MCPHILIP**, who is in her twenties. (She works as a typist or secretary: she's ambitious in that she wants to better her lot.) A bit tired at the moment, a little dishevelled and not at all happy.*

An air of waiting.

GALLAGHER: (*Thinks he hears something*) Shhhh! ... Anything?

1ST GUARD: (*At the foot of the steps*) Anything?!

2ND GUARD: (*Top of steps*) Anything?!

VOICE: (*Off; a lookout*) No!

2ND GUARD: No!

1ST GUARD: No!

Silence.

MULLIGAN: What d'yiz want me for?

GALLAGHER: What time is it now?

1ST JUDGE: Nearly two a.m.

Leabharlanna Poiblí Chathair Bhaile Átha Cliath
Dublin City Public Libraries

MARY: (*Whispers*) Dan ... Dan. (*She's concerned about Mulligan who is crying again.*)

GALLAGHER: (*Hisses*) Commandant! In here you call me Commandant. (*He paces.*) Where are they? I said half past one, sharp. That dull dumb-witted ox! Stupid of me to let him go when I had him! I should have had him shot six months ago.

MARY: And my brother too?

He ignores her last. A clock, off, is chiming two.

All this talk of shooting. It won't bring back the dead.

GALLAGHER: We don't need you here. You may go home.

MARY: I'll stay.

One of the Judges takes out some sweets, offers them to the others. They refuse. Off, car engine, van engine, approaching, stopping.

VOICE: (*Lookout*) They're comin'!

2ⁿᵈ GUARD: They're comin'!

1ˢᵗ GUARD: They're comin'!

GALLAGHER: Have they got him?

1ˢᵗ GUARD: Have they got him?

2ⁿᵈ GUARD: Have they got him?

VOICE: Yes!

2nd GUARD: Yes!

1st GUARD: Yes!

MULHOLLAND comes in; he's a suspicious and cunning man. In contrast CONNORS, who will come in in a moment or two, is more credulous and idealistic. And GYPO, who will precede Connors, is a big man and obviously capable of great strength. He wears a jacket, muffler, baggy trousers and a hat, which appears to mean a lot to him. (Perhaps this last should be a cap – though he can still refer to it as his hat.)

GALLAGHER: What happened?

MULHOLLAND: (*Is nursing a sore eye*) That bastard!

GALLAGHER: I'm asking why are you late?

MULHOLLAND: He gave me the slip. It took me a while to track him down.

GALLAGHER: Was he near a police station?

MULHOLLAND: No. If I'd had the proper order in the first place.

GALLAGHER: To what?

MULHOLLAND: Shoot him.

GALLAGHER: And deprive ourselves of the – stimulation – this court of enquiry will provide, Bartley?

*GYPO, followed by **CONNORS** and **2nd GUARD**, has come in. He stumbles on the steps and takes **CONNORS** to the floor with him. He loses his hat. He is carrying a bottle and, from the floor, he drains it of its contents. Guns are pointing at him. He swings the empty bottle, playfully dismissing the guns.*

MULHOLLAND: That bastard!

GYPO: Fight any six men of ye!

GALLAGHER: Get up, Nolan.

GYPO: (*Salutes*) Reportin' for duty, Commandant! Where's me hat?

GALLAGHER: On your feet!

GYPO: Where's me – ? Ah! (*He's retrieved it. And rises.*) You'n me, Commandant – What-ho! – we'll put 'em all on the run!

GALLAGHER: Over to that seat.

GYPO: Hello boys! (*He sees Mulligan.*) Hey, Rat, what're you doin' here? Man dear alive, this is no hour of night for a sick man to be out of his bed!

MULLIGAN *does not lift his head,* **GYPO** *looks about the room: the* **GUARDS, MARY McPHILLIP, GALLAGHER** *whispering to the masked* **JUDGES**: *he's trying to regain his faculties.*

(*Whispers*) What's goin' on, Rat?

GALLAGHER: (*Finishes whispering to the* **JUDGES**, *turns*) Sit down, Gypo.

1ˢᵗ JUDGE: The Court of the Revolutionary Organisation of Ireland is now in session. Take Peter Mulligan's statement.

GALLAGHER: Peter Mulligan, give an account of your whereabouts from five p.m. yesterday evening until you were brought here tonight.

MULLIGAN: Whatever it is yiz think yiz want me for, before the Blessed Mother of the Infant Jesus I swear I never left the house tonight except to go to the chapel to say me prayers!

GALLAGHER: Give an account of your whereabouts from five pm until you were brought here at midnight.

MULLIGAN: What's the meanin' of this treatment of a workin' man by yous as is supposed to be out for the freedom of the workin'-class? Can yiz find no better man to arrest an' carry off in the middle of the night than me?

GALLAGHER: A statement of your whereabouts.

GYPO: (*Stands and perhaps laughs*) Statement o' yer whereabouts! (*What he really wants to say is 'What's goin' on?'*)

A **GUARD** *intervenes, gun pointing directly at* **GYPO**. *A dismissive flick of his hand knocks the gun aside.*

Keep back from me!

GUARDS, *unsure of what to do, look at* **GALLAGHER**. *He waves them back and takes* **GYPO** *aside.*

(*Disdainfully*) Guns!

GALLAGHER: Yes. Sit over here.

GYPO: What's goin' on? I'm bein' taken back into the ranks, isn't it?

GALLAGHER: We're verifying the statement you made to us earlier tonight in Ryan's public house.

GYPO: Statement, Ryan's, Commandant! (*Though he can't remember.*)

GALLAGHER: Sit down. We'll have some questions to ask of you in a while.

GYPO: Commandant!

GALLAGHER: Now, Peter Mulligan, can we have your statement.

MULLIGAN: I had a bad pain in me right side most of the day. I had it from the mornin', I have it now, bronchitis, an' I tried to rest but I couldn't on account of a suit I'm makin' for Mick Foley, Mick the carter. It hasta be finished be Tuesday, hasta, on account as how Mick's daughter is getting' married an' –

1ˢᵗ JUDGE: Your movements from five o'clock.

GYPO: (*To himself*) Yakety-yak, clackety-clack...

MULLIGAN: The missus called me from me workroom as usual –

GALLAGHER: This was at five o'clock?

MULLIGAN: Five o'clock. But I couldn't touch the egg, nor the cup of tea itself, so I just sat there an' had the smoke.

GYPO: Five o'clock, yakety-yak, clackety-clack...

*Lights are changing. A clock is chiming five. The **JUDGES** divested of their hoods and overcoats become other characters. (For instance two of the Judges are women.) Similarly, the **GUARDS** are transformed. (This convention of doubling continues throughout the play.) And **MULLIGAN'S VOICE** continues his statement during the transition:*

MULLIGAN'S VOICE: Then I went again to me workroom and I'd only started back on the waistcoat when Charlie Corrigan comes in and says his brother Dave had just got out of jail after bein' on hunger strike for eighteen days. Dave that was thrown in on account of the Slum Rents Agitation. I was always very great with Dave. 'He's upstairs in bed', says Charlie, 'I thought you'd maybe like to say hello'. So up I went...

SCENE TWO

*Louisa's and Katie Fox's room. **LOUISA** is in bed. She's old, dirty and half-crazy. She produces a statue and holds it lovingly to herself.*

LOUISA: Ah, there yiz are me aul flower! Blessed St Joseph, friend o' the crippled worker, sure yer the dacentest aul skin of them all, yiz'll see us all alright yet, won't yiz now? Yiz'll not see yer own devoted Louisa much longer laid up here, yiz'll have me on me feet again soon, able to ply me trade as good as the next woman. Loveen!

The statue swivels in her hands in the direction of the door, as though hearing someone approaching.

(*Whispers*) Well, d'yiz know, yiz're better nor a watchdog. (*Putting the statue away:*) But go back yous in there now an' be thinkin' of what I'm askin'. It's Mattie Quinn is comin' up the stairs cause today is Friday, an' it's time for me to earn a bob or two. Who's that, who's that, is that you Mat?

KATIE: (*Off/entering*) 'Tis, 'tis me, 'tis Mat!

KATIE FOX is pretty, in her twenties, but the ravages of her profession have taken their toll. There is an energy and aggression in her laughter and speech. And like LOUISA, she too is on drugs.

'Is that you, Mat?' What year was Mat, or any other Mat, in here with you last? Where's me man? Gypo! Jasus, still asleep, five o'clock in the day.

And indeed, GYPO is lying on the floor (at the foot of the bed), an old blanket around him. He's been staring ahead, at nothing: his future. Now he's pretending to be asleep.

LOUISA: Did yiz bring me nothing home? (*She's eyeing the handbag which KATIE has thrown on the bed. In a moment her hand steals towards the bag.*)

KATIE: Oh, the Dubbelin men don't know what they have it for anymore, an' them that does think they can exercise it for ten-pence hapenny. Touch that bag an' I'll brain yiz!

LOUISA: It's my room, my room, an' yous never give me money.

KATIE: Sorry the day I ever came into your room. Gypo! I'm home.

GYPO: Did yeh get us anythin' t'ate? (*And he will pretend to go back to sleep again.*)

KATIE: Oh, food, food, phoo, phoo!

LOUISA: Yiz got something. Yiz were up in Biddy Burke's an yiz got some of the stuff.

KATIE: Come on Gypo, I'm cold: we'll get into the bed an' go out later on.

LOUISA: She robs me an' she brings me back nothin'.

KATIE: Off the floor, Gypo, come on!

LOUISA: (*Producing a stick*) It's my bed, my bed!

KATIE: If yous don't lie still! Gypo!

LOUISA: My bed!

KATIE: This side here is mine, an' I can let who I like into it!

LOUISA: (*Waving her stick*) Get outa here, yiz dirty pair o' tramps!

KATIE: (*Very threatening*) What did yous call me an' Gypo?

LOUISA: (*Whimpering*) My bed, my bed...

KATIE: Any more now and though it's short yiz are for this world, I'll make it shorter. (*She sits heavily on the bed*)

LOUISA: (*Quietly*) I'll dance on your grave.

KATIE: (*Through this she lies back on the bed*) Though few people know it, me mother was born a lady. Put that in your pipe, Louisa Cummins, an' try to smoke it. Ye've given me nothin' but dog's abuse since I moved into yer rotten room an yiz're not fit to wipe me shoes. So I don't give a damn. An', Gypo, there's a ship in the docks, so I don't give a damn, cause they'll be lettin' the sailors offa it tonight, so I don't give a damn. On the strength of that info, yes, Louisa, I was up in Biddy Burke's an' she gave me a little treat for meself on tick. An' see if I give yiz any of the stuff I'll bring home tonight. Me mother was a rale lady, born in a palace, big as the county of Waterford, an' when I was a little girl ... when I was a little girl ... a little girl ...

She's asleep. **GYPO** *has been waiting his chance: Still on the floor, he knots his muffler, buttons his jacket, ties his bootlaces, punches his hat into shape, crawls to Katie's side of the bed, fumbles under her for her handbag, takes whatever money it contains and steals away. The foregoing while* **LOUISA** *speaks, first having produced the statue again and a piece of string, one end of which – while she speaks to the statue – she ties round the statue's neck, the other end to the top of her stick.* (*To hang the statue*)

LOUISA: Oh ho! Did yiz hear that? An' it's my mother was the rale lady. Sailors offa foreign ships with lavish bags of gold to drive them on, an' me left stranded here: Is that fair? No, but yous'd have me prayin' another thirteen years to yiz here to cure me, would yiz? Yiz're only a gobshite, in one ear out the other! Well there y'are for yiz now! (*She holds up the stick, the statue wildly bobbing from the top of it*) Yiz can hang there till yer dead, an' divil mend yiz! ... (*She grows quiet*) An' sailors, admirals, wouldn't take it but kind to lie with Louisa Cummins one time... until that big blue bastard in his uniform kicked me in the hip for sidin' with the strikers... Oh ho, oh ho...

Lights changing. A clock is chiming the Angelus.

MULLIGAN'S VOICE: (*During the transition*) Then Charlie says, will yiz be staying on a while with Dave, says he: I'd like to go out before the butchers close an' see if there's a few aul bones about to make a drop of soup for him. The hunger strike has left him very weak. I didn't need pressin': stayin on a while with a man as good an' brave as Dave was the least that I could do. 'Twas six o'clock when I left there: the Angelus was ringin' an' I comin' down the stairs again...

SCENE THREE

The Dunboyne Eating-cum-Lodging House.

*GYPO has come away from a serving counter or hatch with a plate of food and sits at a table to eat it. Behind him, at the hatch, an **OLD MAN**, or two – like the top end of a line of down-and-outs – waiting to be served. A man in a cap and shabby raincoat has come in, his movements cautious, one hand in his breast pocket (holding a gun), looking for someone. This is **FRANKIE MCPHILIP**. He's about thirty; he has a haunted – might even be a saintly – look. He has found who he's looking for.*

FRANKIE: Well, Gyp, how's things?

GYPO'S jaws slowly stop working and he looks up at FRANKIE, dumbfoundedly.

I'm not a ghost, aul son.

GYPO: (*In his sudden loud voice*) I know yer not Frankie, but where the divil did yeh come out of?!

FRANKIE: Shhhhh! It don't matter where I come out of, I came in to get wise to all the news.

GYPO: Lord, Frankie, yeh look terrible!

FRANKIE: (*Smiles, he knows it*) What's doin?

GYPO: Nothin'. Nothin' at all. Things is bad. Very, very bad. Not knowin' where the next penny is to come out of. Lord, Frankie, I was just this minute thinkin' there, if I had the price of a bed, a clean bed for one night, one night.

FRANKIE: No, what's the position on me?

GYPO: There's a price on your head!

FRANKIE: Shhhh!

GYPO: Twenty pounds.

FRANKIE: I know.

He starts to cough, the cough shaking his body.

GYPO: Man dear alive, yeh look as if yer dyin'!

FRANKIE: (*Smiles*) That's why I came in, Gypo. Did you deliver my messages?

GYPO: I delivered your messages, Frankie. First to yer mother an' father like yeh said, then to the Executive Committee.

FRANKIE: Yeh?

GYPO: Yer father gave me dogs abuse an' drove me from the house. He cursed you too be bell book and candlelight. But yer mother followed me out, cryin', an' slipped me half a quid to give to yeh. But I'd no way of findin' yeh an' I spent it.

FRANKIE: Doesn't matter.

GYPO: I was hungry, Frankie!

FRANKIE: Shhhh!

GYPO: Things has been terrible –

FRANKIE: Don't mind the money –

GYPO: I had to steal the few coppers for this (*dinner*) offa Katie Fox (a) while ago when I got her sleepin'.

FRANKIE: What about the Executive Committee?

GYPO: Well, I went to the Executive Committee and reported like you told me how to put it.

FRANKIE: Yeh?

GYPO: 'No'! They said we put the whole organization in jipirdy, they said we had no orders to shoot anyone, they said we made an ass's collar out of the whole job, they said there'd have to be a punishment.

FRANKIE: Yeh?

GYPO: Declare to Christ, them two eyes o' Gallagher: Sometimes I think the man is mad. I thought he was goin' to plug me there an' then.

FRANKIE: Yeh?

GYPO: But no, he turns holy, like he do betimes. An' the things I seen that man do when I was his side-kick! There's been enough shootin' for the moment, he says. That what was to be done was a letter to the newspapers, sayin' the Organisation had nothin' to do with that shootin'.

FRANKIE: And what was to be our punishment?

GYPO: That we was disowned, that we was expelled, forever. And that was hard, that was harsh, very, very harsh, to be put out like that, nowhere to go, be left without a friend. No further share in the shillin's, Frankie?

FRANKIE: (*To himself*) Yeh, to be left out there all winter on them hills. To rot. Sleepin' in a hole like an animal, the cold and the damp, starvin' to death. Yeh. I thought they'd want me more than the police: (to) interrogate me, plug me, (or) whatever. I thought Gallagher was sure to come after me. Why didn't he?

GYPO: Well, maybe it's as how yer sister was down a few times to him, lookin' to find out about yer whereabouts, and they say it's as how Gallagher it puttin' the eye on her.

FRANKIE looks up, fiercely.

Oh, but a haughty girl, the sister, and will have no truck, they say, with Gallagher's schemin's, like another girl would.

FRANKIE: What do I care for Gallagher or the Executive Committee? Curse of hell on the lot of them for a pack of whores, whoremasters and robbers! I don't want ever to hear anything more about them.

He is coughing again, his frame shaking.

GYPO: Yer sick, Frankie.

FRANKIE: The police: Did they question you?

GYPO: Did they question me? Did-they-question me! They pulled me in – they pulled in half the town! The threatenin's an' questions! But I had the alleyby (*alibi*) you'd made out for me.

FRANKIE: Wish there could have been an alibi for myself.

GYPO: But they kept on: Where was you, that they know 'twas you done the shootin', that they'd get yeh, one way or another, dead or alive. The rascals! I wouldn't care much for your task then, says I. Did I know – Did-I-know! – The Farmers Bank had put a price on yer head? Did I know...

A thought has entered his head: he can't figure out what it is. He is staring at **FRANKIE.**

FRANKIE: What is it, Gyp?

GYPO: Did I know, could I help them? – Me, Frankie, help the police! So then they gev me a good kickin' an' threw me out.

FRANKIE *chuckles, then* **GYPO** *laughs.*

Aw, you'n me was a great team, we done some stunts together, you doin' the thinkin' an' the alleybyin' an' me doin' the, the...What! (*He can't remember what his contribution was*)

FRANKIE *chuckles.*

Have a bite, comrade, 'twill warm you up. Aw, Frankie, man dear, we had some sport!

FRANKIE *nibbles at a piece of food without much interest in it. He's very gentle now, his eyes on the table. And* **GYPO** *watches him, his brow furrowing, still trying to figure the thought that has entered his mind.*

FRANKIE: I couldn't stand bein' up in the hills anymore. I know the cops are after me, Gyp, I know there's a price on my head, but I don't much mind. I've still got this (*the gun in his breast pocket*), and I don't much mind how I use it. On myself too if needs be. I often think of it. I think I'm ready. So I came down to see my mother. (*He looks up*) Is there a guard on the house?

GYPO: Divil a guard!

GYPO is surprised at the immediate and positive nature of his own reply. He now realizes what has been puzzling him. His eyes dilate, his hand stretches out to touch FRANKIE'S sleeve, as if to deter him from going home.

FRANKIE: What is it Gyp? (*Smiles.*) What's up with you?

GYPO: Yeh see – yeh see, I haven't been near Titt Street, nor next or near yer father's house since the night I went there with your message an' he told me never to darken the door again! Yeh see – yeh see, there's maybe a guard on it an' there's maybe there isn't but – yeh see, yeh see – if you was to go there now and get nabbed – yeh know – yeh see?!

FRANKIE: What are you talking about?

GYPO: Nothin'!

FRANKIE: What?

GYPO: Nothin' at all! It's how you've come up on me so sudden: that's what I'm talkin' about!

FRANKIE: Shhhh!

GYPO: An' I don't know right what I'm thinkin'. D'yeh understant me now? I'm all mixed up these past six months, wanderin' around, without a mate'd lend us a tanner, nowhere to flop down unless it's beside that Katie Fox – (*He breaks off, his head rolling in frustration and disgust:*) Katie Fox, Katie Fox, an' that other aul wan in the bed, lyin' there – the filth, the smells, the things they do be sayin', doin', and takin' that dope they gets in Biddy Burke's – Lord Christ tonight, the pigs in their pigsty is gentlemen to them!

FRANKIE: Easy!

GYPO: An' people is sayin' I'm a – I'm a – Tck-tck! – (*The word embarrasses him:*) pimp. Others sayin' that I'm Katie Fox's an' the aul wan's – Tck! – fancy man. An' the thoughts of goin' back there again tonight! But where else can I (go) unless I'm to die of the cold lyin' in the street with a foot of frost on the ground. So d'yeh see me predicimint? (*He starts to eat hurriedly.*)

FRANKIE: Where did all this gab come from? And 'predicament'?! Are you going to university now in your spare time?

GYPO looks at him, doglike; a weary plea on GYPO'S face for the temptation to be taken away.

So there's no guard on the house?

GYPO: Yer not playin' games with me, are yeh, Frankie?

FRANKIE smiles and shakes his head.

'Cause what I wouldn't give for a sleep in a clean bed.

FRANKIE: I can understand that, Gyp.

GYPO: Well, alright then, lemme see. I know they had two of them watchin' the place till Christmas; then they took them off; then, far as I know, they didn't put them back on again, but a fella, I'm told, goes round now and again to make a few enquiries.

FRANKIE: That's grand. Anything else?

GYPO: (*Eating heartily*) God only knows who's givin' information to the Government now. Yeh never know who you're talkin' to. Tell yeh what, the workin' class ain't worth fightin' for. I think they think yer gone to America. (*He is mopping up his plate*)

FRANKIE: (*Stands*) It's a rotten aul world, Gypo. I'll see you again. (*He leaves.*)

GYPO: So long, Frankie.

*As the lights are changing, a **POLICEMAN** strolls by, as along a street; now that he's passed by, **FRANKIE** appears and moves off in one direction, in and out of shadows. And now **GYPO** comes out of the shadows to take the direction which follows the **POLICEMAN**. An old **PROSTITUTE** moves in and out of the shadows, looking for trade. And **MULLIGAN'S VOICE** over:*

MULLIGAN'S VOICE: Then I got me hat an' overcoat an' the missus got hers: she to go to work, me to the chapel like I always do. She works the nights in Cooney and Kelly's offices, cleanin', and the steps to be done outside. I'm makin' a novena for... It's no one's business but my own who I'm makin' it for...

*Another change of lights (Passage of time.) A clock somewhere is chiming eight. The place/street seems deserted. **GYPO** returns in a furtive way. And is he being followed he wonders. Considering himself to be alone, he produces what appears to be a roll of money. He separates a single note from the roll. Then he is suspended in the action of putting the roll away again by the sudden thought:*

GYPO: Alleyby! Isn't that what I need now?

OLD PROSTITUTE: What d'yiz need, duckie? Anythin' good?

*She has appeared, as out of nowhere, at his elbow. And he's gone. She cackles a laugh and as she disappears again, **KATIE FOX** arrives, with her handbag. She's angry, she's looking for someone (**GYPO**), she's making enquiries...*

SCENE FOUR

*A pub and the street immediately outside it, where a **STREET MUSICIAN** comes along, singing and playing 'Kevin Barry'.*

***PUBLICAN**, behind the counter, is pulling a pint, which **GYPO** has just called for. Nearby is a **SMALL MAN** who would engage **GYPO** in conversation, casting sidelong glances up at **GYPO**. **GYPO** wants none of him. (**GYPO** wants peace and quiet so that he can think.) A clock chimes the half hour.*

SMALL MAN: ... Half eight, wha'?... Wha'? ... (*Referring to the street musician*) Kevin Barry, wha'?... 'Another martyr for aul Ireland,'wha'?

GYPO: Yis.

SMALL MAN: 'Another murder for the crown', wha'? (*He calls after the street musician.*) Oi, segosha, the troubles are over, the topic is changed!

PUBLICAN: Now mister, pint.

GYPO: Thank you. (*He gives a pound note to **PUBLICAN**.*)

SMALL MAN: Wha'?

GYPO: Yis.

SMALL MAN: But what's the use in talkin', sure, wasn't there a man shot dead be the polis, not an hour ago, 'cross the river in Titt Street: Did yiz hear that, wha'?

GYPO: (*Hisses*) I didn't hear! I didn't! Now shut yer gob! Can't a man have a drink in peace?

SMALL MAN: Wha'?

***GYPO** moves away to sit on his own, to think, but **KATIE FOX** arrives.*

KATIE: There yiz are at last! Nellie Mac was right thinkin' 'twas you she spotted crossin' the bridge.

SMALL MAN: Wha'?

KATIE: Well, have yeh spent it all?

GYPO: Spent? Spent what?

KATIE: Yaa! Waitin' to get me sleepin' to slope off with me earnin's.

GYPO: Sure all yeh had in yer bag was tenpence hapenny.

KATIE: There! I caught yiz.

SMALL MAN: Wha'?

GYPO: (*Embarrassed*) Aw, Katie –

KATIE: Yeh pug nose yeh! –

PUBLICAN: No trouble now! –

KATIE: Pug nose! –

GYPO: (*Whispering*) If yeh don't stop I'll –

SMALL MAN: Wha'? –

GYPO: I'll – I'll – I'll –

KATIE: Pug nose! –

GYPO: Hit yeh!

PUBLICAN: D'yiz hear what I'm tellin' yiz?!

KATIE: This thievin' red-neck thick of a Tipperary bastard!

PUBLICAN: Language now, me lady, or you'll feel the fong of my boot on your arse out the door! Now, your change, mister! (*He bangs it on the counter.*)

She registers the amount of change.

KATIE: What's this? Yous have another woman!

GYPO: (*Whispering*) I – tck-tck-tck! – haven't!

KATIE: So yiz don't want to know me when yer in the shillin's, but it's a different story when yiz haven't a tosser: 'Katie darlin', let me in'.

GYPO: Alright, here's – here's –

KATIE: Me keepin' yiz goin' when no-one else in town would give yous the time of day –

GYPO: Here's yer tenpence hapenny back an' off to the divil with yeh.

KATIE: I don't want me tenpence hapenny back. (*She's trying to see how much money he has.*)

GYPO: Will yeh stop, will yeh, with yer spyin' eyes!

KATIE: (*Quietly*) How much have yiz?

GYPO: (*Opens his mouth to speak, claps it shut, and again. Then*) Katie Fox! It's just like yeh to go takin' a man up wrong, it's just like to – What're yeh havin'?

KATIE: Double gin.

GYPO: (*Calls*) Double gin, Boss! (*Reassuring* **PUBLICAN:**) 'Tis alright, there'll be no trouble.

KATIE: Oh, yer a bum alright, Gypo. (*Smiling to herself.*)

GYPO: Stop now, Katie. Don't be – don't be – whist!

KATIE: As soon as yiz hear the jingle in yer rags yer friends are all forgot, pug nose higher in the air.

GYPO: What brought you over here anyways? (*He gives her her drink.*)

KATIE: Oh, yous own this place, do yiz? Well, is that a fact now?

GYPO: Will yeh stop! Haven't I bought yeh a drink?

She holds her glass upside down: She's knocked it back already.

KATIE: Go on tell us, how much have yiz?

GYPO: (*Opens his mouth, nothing comes, claps it shut. Then:*) Shut yer gob! (*And calls:*) Throw us out another pint an' a gin!

KATIE: (*Reassuring **PUBLICAN***) No trouble, Boss, no trouble!

GYPO: (*Does not like taking money out in front of her*) Sit over there.

*The **PUBLICAN** is looking dubious about doing another drink for them. **GYPO** produces another pound. **PUBLICAN** still looks dubious.*

An' have one yourself. An' give one to-to – to the little man.

SMALL MAN: Wha'?

PUBLICAN: A double gin? (*Meaning for Katie*)

GYPO: No – yis!

PUBLICAN: What, which?

GYPO: A double, a double, twill keep her quiet, it always do. (*He stands by waiting for the drinks.*)

PUBLICAN: (*Filling drinks*) You were sayin', Jem?

SMALL MAN: Wha'?

PUBLICAN: Who was shot?

SMALL MAN: Man be the name of McPhilip in Titt Street. I met a man was goin' over there to the wake, to sympathise with the family.

PUBLICAN: An' what would be behind that?

SMALL MAN: The shootin'?

PUBLICAN: Yes.

SMALL MAN: Oh now! (*Shrewdly*)

PUBLICAN: Well, d'yeh tell me so?

SMALL MAN: Oh now!

*GYPO takes drinks to **KATIE**. He sits bolt upright, desperation in his eyes.*

KATIE: D'yeh know what I'm goin' to tell yiz? (*She hooks her arm affectionately into his.*)

GYPO: Shhh! Have to think, Katie.

KATIE: Yeh needn't be lookin' for anythin' offa me anymore for it'll be no use to yiz. (*She giggles.*) What's up, kiddo?

GYPO: (*Sighs*) A plan.

KATIE: A what?

GYPO: Alleyby.

KATIE: Don't mind what I do be sayin' sometimes, because, even if yiz are a pug nose, yiz're the finest man in all Dublin, an' I'm proud o' yiz, so there!... It's nice on our own Gypo. But the world is so hard sometimes. Misery, misery... Even when we're laughin'... Buy us another wet an' we'll go back (*to*) our own side 'cross the river.

GYPO: Have to think first, Katie. (*A whisper to himself.*)

KATIE: No one has pity on no one but themselves. Why is that?... Because no one has nothin'. An' God is no use, 'cause he has no more than anyone else. We know that since you'n'me were communists once in the Organisation.

GYPO: (*Stands suddenly; his sudden, loud voice*) Curse o' hell on him anyway! (*He becomes aware of the others staring at him. He turns on Katie.*) What's that?! None o' that talk about God, lave God out of it! (*To the others:*) What are the Jackeens watchin'?! (*To Katie.*) If you was a bit bigger I'd give you a good skelp! (*Sits abruptly.*) Don't know what I was tryin' to think of now.

PUBLICAN: Alright, that's enough, clear off, the pair of ye, back to yere own side! This is a respectable area and this is a respectable house.

GYPO: (*On his feet*) What's that!

KATIE: It's so respectable it's empty!

GYPO: (*A challenge to fight*) Yis?! (*He drinks back his pint defiantly.*)

KATIE: Come on Gypo, we'll *tear* ourselves away from here!

GYPO: (*Another challenge to fight*) Yis?!

PUBLICAN: Alright, I'm gonna call the civic guards.

GYPO: No need for that. Just, just watch yer manners in future! (*He leaves the pub.*)

KATIE: Yous is only a pair of dried-up aul south-side bollixes anyway!

SMALL MAN: Wha'?

Outside the pub, to himself:

GYPO: Alleyby!

KATIE: (*Joins him; she's laughing*) I knew yiz were yella. Where'd yiz get all the money? Did yiz rob a church?

GYPO: (*Opens his mouth, nothing comes, claps it shut. Then inspiration:*) Rob? Wasn't a church. It was a sailor, sailor off a foreign ship, I went through him at the back of Cassidy's in Jerome Street: What d'yeh think o' that?

KATIE: How much did yiz get?

GYPO: Never you mind, but if you say a word to anyone you know what you'll get.

KATIE: What yiz take me for, an informer? Come on, we'll go back to our own side and up to Biddy Burke's an' you'll buy us a sniff.

GYPO: I won't.

KATIE: Aaa –

GYPO: I'll go near no Biddy Burke's, an' it's that stuff you gets off Biddy has you worse then the aul one at home in the bed.

KATIE: Only for a few drinks then – all the crowd'll be there.

GYPO: I don't want to see the crowd.

KATIE: Aaa!

GYPO: I won't!

KATIE: Where'll we go then? Yous'll look after me, Gypo, won't yiz?

GYPO: I'm goin' down to the Dunboyne to book myself a bed.

KATIE: A bed?

GYPO: (*Telling himself*) Yis, that's it: I robbed a sailor an' now I'm goin' to get meself a bed.

KATIE: Haven't I a bed?

GYPO: Yeh haven't!

KATIE: Yiz don't want me bed, is it? –

GYPO: Yeh haven't -

KATIE: But yiz were glad enough to get it –

GYPO: Yeh haven't -

KATIE: When I took yiz in like a drownded rat! –

GYPO: Yeh haven't, yeh haven't an' I'll give yeh nothin' for your imperence – so there! You're too ignorant, that's what y'are!

KATIE: So I'm not good enough for yiz now, is it?

GYPO: Yer not – an' yer too small – an' yeh have no sense. Me mind's made up.

KATIE: (*Clenched fist under his chin; hisses*) Yaa, pug nose, I'll get yous!

*She walks away, furiously. A moment of regret from **GYPO**, to call her back, give her some money... but it can't be done, Then, the sudden thought strikes him:*

GYPO: Well, amn't I the awful fool! How didn't I think of it! They'll be wonderin' why I'm not there, me that was his best pal.

Lights changing. Figures emerging, people converging on the McPhilip home to sympathise with the McPhilip family.

*Over the transition, **MULLIGAN'S VOICE**:*

MULLIGAN'S VOICE: When I left the chapel I met Fr. Conroy outside the gates an' we stood talkin'. Then Barney Kerrigan came along an' stopped with us. We talked about the Grand National. Then Barney walked me home to me own front door an' I went in. I tried to do another bit of work on the waistcoat of the suit for Mick Foley but...

SCENE FIVE

The McPhilip house and the street outside.

*The McPhilip family: **MOTHER** (Delia), **FATHER** (Jack), **MARY** (whom we've met in Scene One) and (optional) **UNCLE MICK**, an invalid, never speaks, a frightened* *creature, old coat pulled tightly over a nightshirt, bare ankles and shins over old shoes.*

*Some neighbours have arrived, others are arriving. Also present are **GALLAGHER, MULHOLLAND** and **CONNORS**; they are keeping their presence as discreet as possible.*

*There's a bed or, say, a door placed on trestles as for a corpse: 1st **WOMAN** is lighting two candles which are placed on either side of it.*

1ˢᵗ WOMAN: Poor Frankie. An' though we don't have the corpse, it's nicer, more proper, d'yiz know, that the candles is lit.

***MOTHER** starts to weep. They comfort her:*

2ⁿᵈ WOMAN: There, there, now, Delia.

1ˢᵗ WOMAN: There, there, now, a stór.

2ⁿᵈ WOMAN: He's in a better place now, sure.

***MARY** is meeting two more sympathizers at the door: Call them **MR** and **MRS FOLEY**. Usual handshakes etc.*

MRS FOLEY: Poor Frankie, Mary. We only heard it (a) while ago.

MR FOLEY: Mary.

MARY: Thank you for calling. Come in. (*She ushers them to her father.*) Mrs Foley and Mr Foley, Daddy.

MRS FOLEY: I'm sorry for your trouble, Jack.

FATHER: Thanks, Winnie.

MR FOLEY: Jack.

FATHER: Thanks, Stephen.

MARY: Mrs Foley, Mam.

***MOTHER** is in tears again.*

MRS FOLEY: Delia, Delia! God'll look after Frankie for yiz now. God is good to his own.

MARY: (*Goes to her father*) Daddy, will I go out and get a few things?

FATHER: What things?

MARY: A drop of whiskey, a drop of port wine.

FATHER: For what?

MARY: For our guests.

FATHER: Guests? Are we celebratin' something here tonight, have we something to be proud of?

He leaves the room abruptly. Note: **FATHER** *is angry but trying to contain himself. Also he resents the presence of the Organisation trio, but he is not without fear of them.*

In reaction to the above between **MARY** *and* **FATHER,** **GALLAGHER** *whispers an instruction to* **MULHOLLAND** *(to go and buy drink) and* **MULHOLLAND** *leaves, purposefully.*

MRS FOLEY: (*Indicating the empty bed: 'Where's the corpse?'*) But where is...?

1st WOMAN: They took him away.

MOTHER: What use can he be to them now that he's dead?

1st WOMAN: That'll be regulations.

MOTHER: And I pleaded with them.

2nd WOMAN: Isn't Father Conroy gone to see what can be done?

MOTHER: What more can they want of my son?

2nd WOMAN: Father Conroy'll get him back for yiz.

MRS FOLEY: Poor Frankie.

MOTHER: An' he was only skin an' bone.

1st WOMAN: Not a pick on him, Delia, you were sayin'.

2nd WOMAN: An' the cough.

MOTHER: That cough.

1st WOMAN: (*To Mrs Foley*) She barely recognized him.

MOTHER: At first he said he'd only stay the minute, but 'twas me wouldn't let him go. Not that he needed much persuadin'. He was so tired. 'Will you bring me me supper, ma, up to me in bed?'

MRS FOLEY: But couldn't they have arrested him?

1st WOMAN: He tried to escape.

MOTHER: That was the last I heard him say; 'Will you bring me ...'

1st WOMAN: Out the winda.

2nd WOMAN: Upstairs.

1st WOMAN: But the house was surrounded.

2nd WOMAN: A bullet from his own gun they said.

1st WOMAN: That he shot himself.

MRS FOLEY: Poor Frankie.

GALLAGHER and *CONNORS* *have come forward,* *FATHER* *returns to the room.*

CONNORS: Your son was a very brave man, Mrs McPhilip.

GALLAGHER: All who knew him admired him.

CONNORS: What time did he arrive here this evening, Mrs McPhilip?

MOTHER: It must have been comin' up to seven cause Mary was only in the door from work. Isn't that right, Mary?

CONNORS: And what time did the police arrive?

MOTHER: He'd hardly had that raggy raincoat offa him and gone up the stairs when we heard the detective-sergeant bangin' on the door an' callin' out the house was surrounded.

CONNORS: And what exactly did –

FATHER: What's the reason for these questions?!

GALLAGHER: No reason. Our deepest sympathy.

CONNORS: Your son was one of the best, your son was a great man.

GALLAGHER nods to CONNORS to retire with him; then he tells CONNORS to remain in the house while he goes out to the street. (He probably knows that MARY will follow him.) And, again, FATHER has left the room for another part of the house.

MARY comes out to the street, to look up and down: no sign of GALLAGHER. He's watching her, impassively, from the shadows. And when she has given up and is about to return to the house:

GALLAGHER: How's things?!

MARY: What are you doing here? (*She is being cold with him.*)

GALLAGHER: I came to pay my respects.

MARY: Really?

GALLAGHER: And to see you.

MARY: I'm sure.

GALLAGHER: Come over here.

She gestures/shrugs: 'Why on earth should she?' She stays put.

I haven't seen you in a while.

MARY: The reason I sought you out was on my mother's behalf: she wanted to find out where my brother was.

GALLAGHER: (*He approaches her*) And I thought you had a regard for us, a secret sympathy for our work?

MARY: If I had, I've something better to do now.

GALLAGHER: A decent job.

MARY: Is there something wrong with 'a decent job'?

GALLAGHER: (*Sighs*) Mary – Mary! You're a hard woman... When were the police here last?

MARY: (*Shrugs*) Christmas, before Christmas? Why the questions?

GALLAGHER: Bit of a coincidence then their calling tonight, don't you think? I have to check it out. Did you talk to him?

MARY: To whom?

GALLAGHER: Your brother.

MARY: I did.

GALLAGHER: About what?

MARY: That is none of your business. I told him what-I-thought-of-him!

GALLAGHER: Did he say he talked to anyone?

MARY: He talked to Gypo Nolan in some 'eating house' or other – The Dunboyne.

GALLAGHER: Natural enough that he'd look up Gypo. Anybody else?

MARY: I don't know.

GALLAGHER: We'll find out. Did he have papers on him?

MARY: I doubt it.

GALLAGHER: Doubt is no good.

MARY: Well! (*Meaning: 'Well, it'll have to do, won't it?'*)

GALLAGHER: We'll find out at the inquest tomorrow. (*And in reaction to her surprise at his knowledge:*) Yes, it's tomorrow, four o'clock.

MARY: ... Anything else? (*Meaning, cynically, 'May I go now?'*)

GALLAGHER: You could take his place.

MARY: What place?

GALLAGHER: In the Organisation.

MARY: I didn't know he had a place –

GALLAGHER: Oh no –

MARY: That *you* had expelled him –

GALLAGHER: No! –

MARY: Hah!

GALLAGHER: He disobeyed an order, some action had to be taken: a *temporary* measure that would have been reviewed.

MARY: (*Cynically*) That has me convinced.

GALLAGHER: You are a very intelligent and brave woman and no-one, least of all myself, can but admire your strength. But you hold a number of misconceptions. Your brother – regardless of whatever differences you had with him – *was* one of the best – indeed, if not the best. He was a dedicated and determined revolutionary, with his father's energy and his mother's humanity and kindness. Francis Joseph McPhilip was resolved to bring about change because he hated poverty.

MARY: And so do I. (*She is cracking.*)

GALLAGHER: He was admired, looked up to, esteemed, he was a member of headquarters staff, and, because he was who he was, a discipline by way of temporary expulsion had to be imposed on him for his lapse.

MARY: (*Is holding back her tears*) I just want to get out of these slums.

GALLAGHER: Your brother hated the slums. But he wasn't just thinking of himself: he thought of all the people who have to live in them. He thought about the people who created them and who perpetuate them. We won't forget him. I won't forget him. Disagree with him if you will, but respect him. Your brother's aspiration was not for his own personal advancement.

MARY: I don't think I'm being selfish in wanting what I want. (*She is crying, shivering a little.*)

GALLAGHER: I'm sorry, but those things had to be said. (*He makes as if to leave.*)

MARY: Don't go.

GALLAGHER: Come over here.

He goes to the place in the shadows where he stood at the top of this section. And she follows.

MARY: When he came home this evening I hardly recognised him either. But he belonged around here alright. Sick-lookin', cold, tired, poor. And he had a sort of faint smile. I hated the look of him. I thought it terrible that he looked so gentle. He wanted to talk to me. I wouldn't let him. I told him what I thought of him. And Daddy shouting at him. Now he's dead... He looked so gentle.

GALLAGHER: You're shivering. (*He has put an arm around her. Holds her, as if caring. After a moment or two, as if joking:*) But we're friends, aren't we? That much at least, what?

She nods, drying her tears.

Well, that gives me something to be grateful for!

She laughs.

I've been trying with you, haven't I, on the few occasions we've met?

Impulsively, she kisses him on the cheek.

If I had someone like you in the Organisation.

MARY: Do you think someone informed on my brother?

GALLAGHER: It's a distinct possibility. If someone has, I'll find him. I'll treasure the kiss.

*As he walks off, **MULHOLLAND** is coming in carrying a large cardboard box. (Drink.) **GALLAGHER** whispers to him, 'I'll be up in Ryans.' **MULHOLLAND** continues on into the house. **MARY** delays for a moment or two to compose herself. In the house **MULHOLLAND'S** box is being unloaded of bottles and glasses, and drinks are being passed around:*

MRS FOLEY: There y'are, Delia, yer more in need of it than anyone!

1st WOMAN: Now, Stephen, throw that back yeh!

*Et cetera. Until **FATHER**, who has come in, finds a drink in his hand.*

FATHER: What's this?

2nd WOMAN: A drop of malt for yiz, Jack.

FATHER: Where did this come from?

MRS FOLEY: There's Guinness here too, if you'd prefer, Jack, or – ?

FATHER: Who ordered this?!

MULHOLLAND: It's paid for, it's alright.

*FATHER'S fear of the Organisation – of **CONNORS** and **MULHOLLAND** – is now, perhaps fuelling his anger. **MARY** comes in to find out what the shouting is about.*

FATHER: Who ordered this?! Does a man not have charge of his own house anymore?

MOTHER: Jack, what's the matter?

FATHER: There's people here and I don't know them! –

MOTHER: For the love of God, Jack! –

FATHER: And I don't want to know them! They're not wanted here!

MOTHER: Neighbours and friends come to pay their respects.

FATHER: And they can clear, so they can!

MOTHER: Friends of Francis! –

FATHER: Friends?! Is that what they are? Well, it's in Russia them friends should be where they can act the cannibal as much as they like, instead of leadin' good Irishmen astray! Them and their revolutions – wasters and scoundrels! – we've had enough revolutions!

MOTHER: Aw, Jack, Jack, Jack, Jack, Jack! -

FATHER: Socialists and Communists they call themselves – well I call them tramps! Robbin' an' smugglin' an' murder is their revolution, then off back with them to hide in a hole! -

MARY: What started all this? -

CONNORS: He's objecting to the drink. -

FATHER: Well they're not wanted here! -

1st WOMAN: (*Optional speech*) Uncle Mick is frightened, Jack.

*MR and **MRS FOLEY** are making for the door.*

FATHER: Winnie, Stephen! – Yiz know I'm not talkin' about yous. (*Shouts at **CONNORS** and **MULHOLLAND**:*) I'm not afraid of yiz! In me own home! People in this street tryin' to live decent lives an' better themselves and do the best we can for our children, an' we're the revolutionaries! Yous think yiz're heroes but yiz're only gangsters! Was my son a hero? I slaved to educate my son, I saw that he went into a good job, a job that if he minded it, would see him get on well in life and be able to help them worse off than himself: Instead, he ends up carted away like the carcass of an animal in the back of a van this evenin'. Was he a hero? So pack up yere bloody drink now and get out of here!

CONNORS: We mean no disrespect to you, Mr McPhilip –

FATHER: What?! What?! -

CONNORS: But we are not gangsters! –

FATHER: Don't address me in me own house! –

MULHOLLAND: (*To **CONNORS***) Let it go –

FATHER: Don't you – I'm not afraid of yiz! Just go, g'wan, there's nothing to celebrate here. My son is dead and he is and he was a disgrace.

Silence. Then MARY comes forward to confront her father.

MARY: He wasn't a disgrace.

FATHER: You've changed your tune.

MARY: I didn't agree with him but he had his beliefs and I respect and stand by him for that. He had a greater love than anyone here for humanity because what he did was unselfish.

FATHER: And the man he shot in Mullagh six months ago? –

MARY: My brother will not be forgotten –

FATHER: Was that poor man not humanity too? –

MARY: And if there's blame to be laid at anyone's door for the way my brother died, that too will be settled.

FATHER: You look out, me lady, or maybe you'll be gettin' your comeuppance too. (*He leaves the room.*)

MARY has taken up a drink: She raises her glass, as in a toast, and drinks. Others, as appropriate, drink with her.

*The whisper goes round that **FR. CONROY** is returning. **FR. CONROY** comes in.*

FR. CONROY: We'll say a prayer. I spoke to the authorities, Delia: We'll have his body back tomorrow night. There has to be an inquest. Kneel and we'll say a few decades of the Rosary for Frankie's soul, that God will forgive him his sins and take him to His bosom.

They kneel, FATHER returns and joins in the prayers.

Incline unto mine aid, O God.

OTHERS: O Lord, make haste to help us.

FR. CONROY: Glory be to the Father, the Son and to the Holy Ghost.

OTHERS: As it was in the beginning, is now and ever shall be, world without end, Amen.

FR. CONROY: The Five Sorrowful Mysteries, the first mystery, The Agony in the Garden. Our Father, who art in...on earth as it is in Heaven.

OTHERS: Give us this day our daily... deliver us from evil, Amen.

FR. CONROY: Hail Mary ... fruit of thy womb, Jesus.

OTHERS: Holy Mary ... at the hour of our death, Amen.

Et cetera.

*Outside, **GYPO** has arrived. He's nervous about entering the house. Eventually he comes in. He opens his mouth to speak, then claps it shut. He sits on the side of the bed. Then he remembers he has his hat on, takes it off and stuffs it into his pocket. He kneels on one knee. The prayers continue. Tears are running down his face. He wants to speak.*

FR. CONROY: Hail Mary full of Grace, the Lord is with thee –

GYPO: (*Loud, sudden voice*) I'm sorry for your trouble, Mrs McPhilip!

***FATHER** mutters something. **MARY** comes in.*

MOTHER: Let him alone, Jack. Thanks, Gypo!

FR. CONROY: Blessed is the fruit of thy womb, Jesus –

GYPO: (*His thunderous voice again*) I just dropped in to tell yeh, Mrs McPhilip!

MOTHER: I know that well, Gypo, I know that, son.

OTHERS: Holy Mary, mother of God, pray for us sinners, now and –

GYPO: You were always good to me, Mrs McPhilip, an'-an'-an'- (*He has risen, as to leave.*)

MOTHER: Jack, tell him he's welcome.

GYPO: I won't be upsettin' yeh, Mr McPhilip! I only dropped in to pay me respects!

*He pulls his hat out of his pocket and a shower of coins cascade to the floor. He looks about the room, wildly. **MR FOLEY/SOMEONE** stoops to pick up the coins:*

Lave them alone!

He scoops up some of the coins. Then, on another impulse, he throws back his head and shouts:

I swear before Almighty God, I warned him to keep away from this house!

CONNORS and MULHOLLAND have picked up some coins and come forward to return them to GYPO.

CONNORS: Stop shoutin' man!

GYPO: He was my friend!

CONNORS: We know that!

GYPO: I warned him!

CONNORS: Stop shoutin'!

On another impulse GYPO has elbowed through them to MOTHER. Then he gives her the handful of coins:

GYPO: You were always good to me! I'm sorry for your trouble, Mrs McPhilip!

And he leaves. Outside, he stops to wipe his eyes and to put on his hat. He's about to move off.

MULHOLLAND: Gypo!

MULHOLLAND and CONNORS have come out of the house. MARY follows and stands in the doorway. MULHOLLAND, feigning casualness, joins GYPO. Inside, the rosary continues.

Where's the hurry takin' yiz?

GYPO: What hurry? How do you make out I'm in a hurry?

MULHOLLAND: Don't get the rag out. You might stop and talk to people.

GYPO: What's that?!

MULHOLLAND: We never see yiz at all now since you left us. Are yiz workin'?

GYPO: No, I'm not, no, I'm not.

MULHOLLAND: Are yeh not?

GYPO: No, I ain't workin' an' all you fellas was said to be comrades o' mine take damn good care – damn good care – to keep out of me way for fear I might ask for the price of a feed or a flop.

MULHOLLAND: Jaysus, Gypo, you know we wouldn't see you stuck if we had it ourselves.

GYPO: That's a likely tale, a likely tale, Bartley Mulholland. All the loot the Organisation has, and shares for all! Ye're a right quare lot o' Comminists.

MULHOLLAND: Still, yeh don't seem to be short of money tonight, wha'?

GYPO: (*Opens his mouth, claps it shut. Then:*) What's that?!

MULHOLLAND: Aren't yiz goin' to offer to stand us a wet somewhere?

GYPO opens his mouth again, claps it shut, another moment of hesitation, opens his mouth and, then his hand shoots out and he has **MULHOLLAND** *by the throat.* **MULHOLLAND'S** *fists and arms flail unavailingly.* **CONNORS** *runs to the rescue. An elbow from* **GYPO** *sends* **CONNORS** *flying.*

GYPO is squeezing the life out of **MULHOLLAND**, **CONNORS** *has produced a revolver:*

CONNORS: Are yeh goin' to let him go, Nolan?

MARY: (*Has joined them*) Don't! Let him go, Gypo.

GYPO: (*Releases Mulholland*) He suspects me!

CONNORS: (*Perplexed*) Suspects you of *what*?

GYPO: Of-of-of- He suspects me!

MARY: (*to Mulholland*) Are you alright?

CONNORS: What's up with yeh, man?

GYPO: You don't know him, Tommy –

MULHOLLAND: I only asked him to –

GYPO: Yer a liar! Well I know that, Bartley Mulholland! Suspects me! D'yeh think I don't know yeh and all about yeh? Yer a liar! And the grudge, Tommy, he got again' me and Frankie this while back, jealous o' me an' Frankie, an' nosin' after Frankie's job – that yeh didn't think Intelligence Officer Number Three was good enough for yeh!

CONNORS: Shut up! D'yeh want the dogs in the street to know our business?

GYPO: 'Tis alright, Tommy, I've nothin' again' you.

CONNORS: Then quieten down. (*To Mulholland:*) Are you alright?

MULHOLLAND whispers something to him. CONNORS nods. Then:

Let's all go up to Ryan's pub.

GYPO: What for?

CONNORS: Commandant Gallagher is up there.

GYPO: So what?

CONNORS: Just for a chat.

GYPO: I ain't a member of the Organisation no more so what's he got to do with me?

MARY: He only wants to ask you a few questions.

GYPO: What's that?!

MARY: Because Frankie said he met you.

CONNORS: He won't eat yeh.

MULHOLLAND: Unless it's afraid of him y'are?

GYPO: I ain't afraid of any man was ever pupped! C'mon!

He strides off, **CONNORS** *and* **MULHOLLAND** *following.* **MARY** *hurries into the house, returns with her overcoat and follows them.*

FR. CONROY: First Mass in the morning will be said for the repose of the soul of Frankie McPhilip. Hail Holy Queen.

OTHERS: (*As the lights fade*) Hail, holy queen, mother of mercy, hail our lives, our sweetness and our hope; to thee do we cry, poor banished children of Eve, to thee do we send up our sighs, mourning and weeping in this valley of tears...

INTERMISSION

SCENE SIX

The front room – or snug – of Ryan's pub. **DRINKERS** *and* **GALLAGHER**.

MULHOLLAND *comes in and whispers something to* **GALLAGHER**.

GALLAGHER: Gypo? (*And laughs at the idea of Mulholland's suspicion.*) I've never known Gypo to take an initiative in anything in his life.

MULHOLLAND: Will I bring him in?

GALLAGHER: Okay.

MULHOLLAND: And McPhilip's sister is out there too in the street. She followed us here.

GALLAGHER: Don't look so glum, Bartley. Tell her to wait there.

MULHOLLAND goes out. If other drinkers are present, **GALLAGHER** *has a word with them and, obligingly, they take their drinks elsewhere, off.*

BARMAID: Another drink, Dan?

GALLAGHER: We'll call you when we need you, Kitty.

MULHOLLAND, GYPO and CONNORS come in.

GALLAGHER: Well, Gypo! You don't seem pleased to see me?

GYPO: Can't say that I am, Commandant.

GALLAGHER: Oh?

GYPO: I ain't in the habit of crawlin' on me belly to someone that don't like me.

GALLAGHER: ... You're a queer fish, Gypo.

GYPO opens his mouth to reply, then claps it shut.

What? Are you still holding it against me your being expelled from the Organisation?

GYPO: (*Angrily*) Yis, I'm – I won't say!

GALLAGHER: But be reasonable. What else could you expect? You were sent down the country, to Mullagh, with Frankie McPhilip to look after the defence work of the strikers there. Your orders were simple: Keep off the booze and don't use lead. And what did you do? The very first thing: you got hold of two women – (*And because GYPO is nodding his head angrily:*) What?

GYPO: I won't say.

GALLAGHER: Then you got drunk in the company of these women and –

GYPO: Many's the good man I been out with on other stunts had a taste for that kind o' honey, Commandant?

GALLAGHER: ... Yes. A queerer fish than maybe I imagined. You got so drunk that McPhilip went out *looking* for trouble, he wanted to shoot up the town. You would have been assisting him but for the fact that at this stage you were engaged with a lamp-post, trying to pull it out of the street by its roots for a bet of a quart of stout. What?

GYPO: (*Defiantly*) A gallon.

GALLAGHER: Yes. In the middle of this – entertainment – McPhilip met the secretary of the Farmer's Union and shot him dead. That utter and incredible piece of stupidity set back, ruined, years of work the Organisation had put in to winning support for itself in rural areas. Then McPhilip hid out, sending you back here to Dublin with a tall story about your being attacked and what not. So what was I to do?

GYPO: So what was you to do!

GALLAGHER: I can tell you, only for me you wouldn't have got away with it as soft as you did. There were others who wanted to give you this.

*He thrusts a gun, which he holds in his pocket, into **GYPO'S** side or back. A moment of hesitation from **GYPO**, then a downwards swing of his fist hitting the gun pressing into him and making **GALLAGHER** totter back from him.*

*Tense moments follow. **GALLAGHER'S** face is dark. The others have their guns at the ready in their pockets. And **MARY** comes in. **GALLAGHER** merely glances at her, he looks at the others telling them to relax. **GYPO** stands there, a man prepared to fight. He laughs at them.*

GYPO: No use tryin' yer tricks with me, Danny Gallagher!

MARY: I've been left standin' out there for –

GYPO: And I know – I know well – if anyone wanted me an' Frankie plugged, I know who that would be! Yeh done it before!

MARY: I'm not accustomed to –

GYPO: And if anyone didn't want us plugged, I might know his reason for that too. (*He glances meaningfully at Mary.*)

MARY: I'm not accustomed to being left standing about in the street!

CONNORS: I'll take her home, will I?

GALLAGHER: She's with us now. (*To Mary:*) I didn't know you were out there. Sit down. (*He doesn't wait for an answer.*)

She does not know how to handle the situation. She tries to present a sophisticated, public image. She sits.

There is a silence, a deliberate one controlled by **GALLAGHER** (*to unnerve Gypo*). *Then he glances at* **MULHOLLAND**.

MULHOLLAND: Buy us a wet, Gypo.

GYPO: (*Opens his mouth, claps it shut. Then:*) Yer a liar! Jesus Christ, Jesus Christ! An' I done more for the Organisation than any man unhung has done. Jesus Christ! An' the way I've been treated, an' just on account of some aul farmer gettin' plugged. Jesus Christ tonight!

GALLAGHER: (*Calmly*) I'll be buy you a drink, Bartley. Would you like a drink, Tommy? Gypo?

GYPO: What's that?!

GALLAGHER: (*Calls*) Kitty! Four glasses of Jameson! (*Then as if remembering Mary:*) Oh! Would you? (*And not waiting for an answer, calls:*) Make that five! (*To Gypo:*) I'm only trying to clear the air because something serious has come up tonight, something that's as much your business as ours, and we just have to forget any grievances we feel we may hold against each other, because –

GYPO'S finger is up.

Yes?

GYPO: Forgotten.

GALLAGHER: Good. Because –

GYPO: 'Tis all forgot, Commandant.

GALLAGHER: Because we must work together on this one.

GYPO: Commandant!

BARMAID has brought the drink (or she's handing it through a hatch). GALLAGHER sees to the drink, pays for it, hands it around...

Aw, we done some stunts together, the Commandant an' me. Why, I could tell you things, comrades, about him would make the hair stand up on the top of yer head. An' me an' a few o' the boys in the old days, comrades, we'd be jokin about the Commandant, callin' him Father Danny, him bein' only a whisker away from bein' a priest one time. Or maybe you was one. Was you?

GALLAGHER: What'll we drink to, boys?

GYPO: To old times!

MULHOLLAND: Absent friends?

They drink. GYPO knocks his back in one go, looks about for BARMAID as if to call a round, remembers himself and claps his mouth shut.

BARMAID: Your change, Dan.

GALLAGHER: The same again, Kitty!

GYPO: (*Chuckles*) Father Danny!

GALLAGHER: (*To the others*) He did do a lot for the Organisation – (*To* **GYPO**) You did do a lot for us – (*To the others*) And he's had a rough time of it for the past six months, paid his penalty for his part in that Mullagh business – (*To* **GYPO**) so, I'm going to have the expulsion order against you reviewed, I'm going to see that you're taken back into the Organisation, on condition –

GYPO'S hand shoots out for a handshake.

On condition –

GYPO: Yeh won't regret it.

GALLAGHER: On condition that you do everything in your power to help us track down the man who informed on Frankie McPhilip.

CONNORS: Your pal.

MULHOLLAND: You were probably the last one to see him before he went home.

GALLAGHER: Can you think of anything that might help us?

GYPO: (*Has been frowning, as in deep thought. He looks up.*) Informer?

GALLAGHER: Has to be. Too much of a coincidence: Frankie down from the hills after months of hiding, same evening, after a long absence, the police are around the house.

The second tray of drinks has been delivered. **GYPO** *marches to the tray, looks back at* **GALLAGHER** *for permission to take a drink.* **GALLAGHER** *nods.*

GYPO: Thank you. (*And drinks.*)

GALLAGHER: Did Frankie mention anything that sounded strange, or of special interest? ...Did you see anything that looked suspicious? ...Was there anyone -

GYPO'S finger is up.

Yes?

GYPO: Permission to go to the cassy, Commandant?

GALLAGHER nods and GYPO marches out. CONNORS follows.

CONNORS: I must go myself.

MULHOLLAND: It's him!

BARMAID: It'll soon be drinking-up time, gentlemen. Dan?

GALLAGHER: Tell the governor I'll be staying on a while. *Keep the change, and I don't want to be disturbed.*

BARMAID looks angry, a glance at MARY, closes shutters (or bangs down the hatch) to this part of the pub.

MARY starts to rise. GALLAGHER restrains her – a gentle touch on her shoulder, without looking at her, so that she sits again. (He has been doing things like this – a touch to her shoulder, hair, hand – as if caring of her.) She's out of her depth.

MULHOLLAND: You know it's him!

GALLAGHER: Are you telling me what I think?

MULHOLLAND: It's him.

GALLAGHER: And what do you want to do? Deal with the matter *here*: a skirmish in a pub? We've had to deal with a spy or two in the past, an informer, and how our methods of dealing with them are remembered.

MULHOLLAND: What do we do if he walks out of here? That's what he thinks he's going to do. Are you going to stop him, without a gun?

GALLAGHER: You are going to follow him.

MULHOLLAND: And if he goes near a police station? He seems to have a lot of dope on you.

GALLAGHER: (*Laughs, lightly, for* **MARY'S** *benefit*) Of course, *then*, you would have to shoot him, Bartley.

MARY: Please stop this.

GALLAGHER: (*Tells her*) It's alright: There will be a proper Court of Inquiry, presided over by members of the Executive Committee and a judgement made.

MARY: I'd like to go home.

A gentle touch to her hand from **GALLAGHER** *by way of reply. And, off, laughing,* **GYPO** *is returning, followed by* **CONNORS.**

GYPO: (*Off and as he enters*) Hurry up, Tommy, don't be dallyin'! (*Salutes*) Commandant! (*Then proceeds to the tray of drinks and downs a drink.*)

GALLAGHER: It's getting late, Gypo. Is there any clue you can give us that might lead us to the man who informed on Frankie McPhilip?

GYPO: More than a clue, Commandant.

GALLAGHER: Yes?

GYPO: Your word holds good about taking me back?

GALLAGHER: Yes?

GYPO: It was Rat Mulligan. It was the Rat Mulligan informed, as sure as Christ was crucified.

CONNORS: Rat Mulligan? Peter Mulligan the tailor?

GYPO: Yis.

MULHOLLAND: How d'yiz make that out?

GYPO: Well, I'll tell ye. I didn't like sayin' anything before because, God knows, it's a quare charge to bring again' anyone, but seein' as how ye put it, it bein' me duty, Frankie bein' me pal an' all, an' –

MULHOLLAND: Come on, man, finish what yiz have to say!

GYPO: What's that?! (*Glares at **MULHOLLAND** and then takes up another drink by way of defiance.*) This is how is was. Soon as Frankie left me at the Dunboyne, I said to myself what the man is doin' is foolish. How I'd been tellin' him not to go next or near home or Titt Street! So I goes out, thinkin' I'll give him one last shout. But he was down the lane across the street an' nearly turnin' the corner. Then I thinks, let him off, he only wants to see his mother. Then I sees, in an out of the shadows, now tight by this side of the lane, now the other, the Rat followin' – A blind person would know the shape an' cut of that man! It's as clear as daylight, so it is!

GALLAGHER: You'll have to do better than that.

GYPO: (*Giving thanks to the ceiling*) How didn't I think of it before!

GALLAGHER: How didn't you think of what before?

GYPO: The grudge.

GALLAGHER: What grudge?

GYPO: The grudge he had in for Frankie! (*He glances at the two remaining drinks:*) Commandant?

GALLAGHER: Go ahead.

GYPO: Well, seein' as no one else is makin' much use of it. Good health! (*Downs the drink.*)

GALLAGHER: The grudge.

GYPO: Well, yeh remember the Rat had a daughter, Susie? (*Grins.*) Aw, why wouldn't yeh remember her, Commandant! Susie!

GALLAGHER: What about her?

GYPO: Well she had a baby, didn't she? And Frankie was said to be the father, they said. Didn't they?

GALLAGHER: Get on with it.

GYPO: Many's the time I'd see them jawin' away, Frankie and Susie, at the back of Cassidy's pub, she cryin' an' askin' him to take her away somewhere. An' the Rat an' his missus up an' down to Frankie's house, cryin' and bawlin' – An' the priest, Fr. Conroy, was in on it. But would Frankie hell budge for any of them, would Frankie hell be the one caught for it!

GALLAGHER: (*To Mary*) Is this true? Was there trouble between your families?

MARY: Yes.

GYPO: Yis! Soon after, as I think yeh know, Susie took the boat over to the 'Pool. Last I heard, she'd went on Lime Street, the creature. (*Prepares to leave.*) Well, Commandant, your promise of reinstatement I know will hold good.

GALLAGHER: There will be a Court of – a court about the matter tonight. Bartley will take you to the place.

GYPO: Time, Commandant?

GALLAGHER: Half one.

GYPO: Rely on me. I'll be outside Sligo Cissy's, Bartley, at one an' I'll see yeh there.

MULHOLLAND: Right y'are. Oh, Gypo, d'yeh mind tellin' me where yeh got the money I seen yiz with tonight?

*GYPO glares at **MULHOLLAND** , claps his mouth shut, then whispers in **GALLAGHER'S** ear.*

GALLAGHER: An American sailor, was it?

GYPO is stumped for a minute, then a bovine nod.

That's great. Yeh know, Gypo, the Government would give a lot more than a twenty pound reward for information on me.

GYPO: The rascals! (*He takes up the remaining untouched drink, and:*) To absent friends, comrades: to Frankie, one decent, sound, brave man and soldier, yer brother, miss, we was very close!

He knocks back the drink, slaps down the glass, clicks his heels, salutes and exits. Off, we hear him give a whoop, celebrating himself.

GALLAGHER: Stick to him like glue, note down everything you see, mobilize whoever you need, but have him at the Bogey Hole at half one sharp.

***MULHOLLAND** exits.*

(*To **CONNORS:***) Contact Hackett, tell him to inform the Executive Committee that there is a Court of Inquiry tonight and judgement to be handed down. Mobilise whoever you need and have this Mulligan at the Bogey Hole, one thirty, sharp. Wait a minute. Delegate one of your men to check on Gypo's movements, say from half five this evening, who he's been with, if he's spent any money, *anything* about him.

***CONNORS** exits. A great deal of inner excitement is going on in **GALLAGHER**. **MARY** appears petrified. She whispers:*

MARY: Take me home.

GALLAGHER: (*To himself*) Well – well!

MARY: I'm frightened.

GALLAGHER: The fun is starting. You must attend the Court of Inquiry too tonight. (*His arm is around her.*)

MARY: Take me home.

GALLAGHER: I'll drain the blood of whoever informed against Francis Joseph McPhilip before dawn.

MARY: Please...please...please

*His other arm is around her, he is kissing her, she is helpless, he's undressing her. Lights changing, **FIGURES** appearing again, as in a street: **OLD PROSTITUTE**, **LOITERERS**, **A SAILOR**, **KATIE FOX**, an **EVANGELIST**...*

MULLIGAN'S VOICE: (*Over the above transition*) About ten o'clock I went upstairs to Jem Daly's room is on the third floor. Jem that's bad with the kidneys these tuthree years, and stayed there havin' the chat till about eleven, when I came down again because that's the time the missus gets in from work. Wasn't long after that – we were gettin' ready for the bed – when Tommy Connors there came in, without as much as by your leave, put a bag over my head and brought me here.

SCENE SEVEN.

*Street scene, after closing time. (There is a fish and chip shop nearby.) Knots of people standing about, reluctant to go to their dreary homes, welcoming of diversion of any kind. An **EVANGELIST** moves among them. They pay little or no attention to him; indeed it is possible that he is not listening to himself; the scene goes on as if he were not there.*

EVANGELIST: What is sin, what is sin? Sin is meanness, sin is smallness, sin is selfish, sin is disobeying the Lord Jesus

Christ, God's only son who died on the cross to save me. Sin is wounding to the Lord Jesus Christ, which I do through my thoughts, words, deeds and omissions, and when I think of what the Lord Jesus Christ did for me, it's clear to me that I'm mean, that I'm small and that I'm selfish. And once a person has died for me, once a person has shed his blood for me, there should be nothing I can decently refuse him. Yet that's exactly what I do, which makes it clear that I'm mean, that I'm small, that I'm selfish. Selfish too in my sins of eating, drinking, smoking, bad language and worst of all in my sins against purity. I speak to the married, the single, those girls of ill repute, young boys and to myself...

Interspersed in the above: A foreign **SAILOR** *has come along:* **OLD PROSTITUTE** *emerges to proposition him. ('Anything good on yer mind, duckie?')* **SAILOR** *sees* **KATIE**, *goes to her and propositions her.*

KATIE: How much did yiz say? Ah, you're takin' the Irish Free State too serious, entirely! (*She walks away.*)

SAILOR: (*Following*) I give two.

KATIE: Aw, God, no, son, I couldn't take two pounds offa yiz!

SAILOR: No! Shilling!

KATIE: Yes, yes, I know, Jesus! Goodnight, tulip!

Off, a celebratory whoop, 'Yahoo!': **GYPO**. *And he enters.* **MULHOLLAND** *follows surreptitiously.*

(*Quietly:*) Yahoo. (*Then:*) Ya-ya, Pugnose! I'll fix you yet! (*To Sailor:*) Okay, kiddo, c'mon! (*As she leaves with Sailor:*) I'll fix that big thick lump of coillte pleb...

BYSTANDERS *are amused, they laugh.* **GYPO** *is moving on, but changes his mind, picks on two young* **MEN**. (*One of the men is eating a bag of chips.*)

GYPO: What are ye lookin' at?

1ST MAN: Nothin'.

GYPO: Yer a liar!

1ST MAN: I'm not.

GYPO: Don't I see yeh lookin' at me?

1ST MAN: I'm not.

GYPO: (*To 2ND MAN*) Is he lookin' at me?

1ST MAN: (*Calls to someone across the street*) Mixer!

2nd MAN: A cat can look at a king.

GYPO: What's that?! What're sayin' about kings? –

2nd MAN: Hold on there –

MIXER: (*Who is probably a boxer*) Something up? –

GYPO: Better say nothin' about kings round here –

1st MAN: Listen to yer man!

GYPO: I think yer lookin' for trouble – Are yeh enjoyin' yer chips? –

MIXER: Something up with yiz, pal? –

GYPO: (*Still feigning to ignore Mixer*) Would yeh enjoy a nice belt in the jaw?

MIXER: I wouldn't try that –

*MIXER'S fist is raised but now, **GYPO**, with a thrust of his elbow, has sent **1st MAN** in on top of him; almost simultaneously he has **2nd MAN** by the scruff of the neck and sent him careening across the street; and there's a gurgling laugh in his throat at the prospect of further physical action.*

*A circle has formed for the fight, which includes a woman who appears to be **MIXER'S MOTHER** and, now, in his apron, an **ITALIAN** fish-n-chip man.*

MIXER: So it's a fight yiz want? Roi? (*Right*)

OTHERS: Get him, Mixer!

Give him what he's lookin' for!

A right good diggin'!

The aul one-two, Mixer!

Flatten him! (*Etc.*)

MIXER'S MOTHER: There's me son, Mixer: Bate the bejasus outa him!

GYPO: Come on then, Mixer, me little prancin', dancin' Jackeen!

Combat is joined. Flurries of fists from **MIXER**, *circling* **GYPO**; *some wild swings from* **GYPO**; **ONLOOKERS** *cheering;* **GYPO** *somehow loses his hat; until* **GYPO** *lands one and* **MIXER** *goes down.*

OTHERS: Up, Mixer!

Get up, Mixer!

And bate the bejaysus out of him, Mixer!

And kick the seven shades of shite out of him, Mixer!

GYPO: (*Scornfully*) Mixer. (*And he laughs. Then, playfully:*) Now where's the little fella with the bag o' chips was talkin' about the king?

But now **MIXER'S MOTHER** *has armed herself with a stick.*

MIXER'S MOTHER: What's he done to me son! By the sweet, livin' an' Holy Virgin Mary, I'll settle him meself!

She's swinging the stick at **GYPO**, **GYPO** *retreating, laughing. Then he catches the stick; then her two hands on it, to wrest it* *back, and his two hands on it, he starts to dance her about the street:*

GYPO: Come on, Granny: One two three, one two three...

*Until she releases her hold of the stick, and gets some kind of missile, a stone: She aims, fires, **GYPO** ducks and the **ITALIAN** fish-n-ship man's great amusement is over because the sound of breaking glass, off, means that the stone has gone through his window.*

ITALIAN: Broka my window!

1ST MAN: Look out, the rozzers is comin'!

*And, with the exception of the **ITALIAN**, all clear, including **MIXER** and **GYPO**, as two **POLICEMEN** arrive.*

1ST POLICEMAN: Hey, ye! Stop! Come back here!

2ND POLICEMAN: What do we have here now?

ITALIAN: Broka my window, broka my window! (*And continues jabbering in Italian*)

*The **OTHERS** who fled are now shouting abuse at the **POLICEMEN** and some missiles are hurled, perhaps.*

OTHERS: (*Off*) Bowsies!

Flat feet!

Shag off!

Rozzers!

Micks! (*Etc.*)

***GYPO** has returned. He has discovered that he has lost his hat. He's moving fast – running perhaps – and laughing, enjoying the motion of his body, circling the **POLICEMEN**, waiting the opportunity to dart in to where his hat is and retrieve it. **OTHERS** are returning to witness this strange spectacle.*

Leabharlanna Poibli Chathair Bhaile Átha Cliath
Dublin City Public Libraries

*GYPO is darting in to his hat; **1st POLICEMAN**, baton drawn, lunges at **GYPO**; a tap on the jaw from GYPO – and a laugh – and **1st POLICEMAN** goes down, falls on top of **GYPO'S** hat. The **OTHERS** cheer. **GYPO** has stooped to get at his hat and **2nd POLICEMAN** has come up behind him and pinned his arms behind his back.*

2ND POLICEMAN: I have yeh now, me fine bucko!

*GYPO marshals his strength, leans forward, heaving **POLICEMAN** on to his back, leans backwards, then forwards, letting **POLICEMAN** go, sending him flying over his head. Then he races off, delighted with himself, the **OTHERS** following, cheering him.*

POLICEMEN picking themselves up:

2ND POLICEMAN: Who is that big mad mullacker?

1ST POLICEMAN: I don't know

ITALIAN: (*Jabbering in their faces:*) Broka my window! (*Etc.*)

2ND POLICEMAN: (*To Italian*) Aw, enough, enough, Jesus! Let's get out of here.

*They leave. The **OTHERS** and **GYPO** return. He is now their hero.*

OTHERS: Long life to yiz!

Up the rebels!

That's the treatment for them! (*The police*)

GYPO: (*Finds his hat*) I thought they might have pinched it. I'd be lost without it. I had it these two years. (*He wears it like a crown. He's smiling on his minions:*) D'ye want to know a secret? Well, before long ye'll see meself an' a – a certain Commandant cocks o' the walk round here. What d'ye think o' that?

OTHERS *are appreciative of it.*

ITALIAN: (*To* **MIXER'S MOTHER**) You broka my window! Who'sa gona pay?

GYPO: Shut yer gob! I'ma gona pay! (*He turns his back on them to separate a pound from his roll and gives it to Italian:*) Here! (*Then, regally:*) Well, I never had such good fun! Are ye hungry? Right, I'm goin' to give every man jack o' ye an' woman that's here a feed o' fish-n-chips. Hey, you, Antonio! Chuck us a feed for all hands.

ITALIAN: Biga lota people.

GYPO: Never you mind about that.

They crowd off to the fish and chip shop. **MULHOLLAND** *emerges from the shadows: He has been registering everything. He moves off, no doubt to take up a new discreet vantage point.*

Lights change for a passage of time. And we are in another part of the street or another street. It appears deserted except for the **EVANGELIST**. *And now, from another direction,* **GYPO** *comes along, finishing a bag of chips. He stops, idly, to listen to* **EVANGELIST**. *It's difficult to tell what, if anything, penetrates, though his chewing on the chips slows down.*

EVANGELIST: Now what is to be done, what is to be done? Well, the first thing is to say I'm sorry. Once I'm really sorry I shall have begun to think of him whom I have betrayed. Once I have confessed I shall have begun to think of the cruel way he died. And my sorrow and confession will lead to forgiveness, to absolution and to love.

A noise somewhere behind **GYPO**. **OLD PROSTITUTE** *has surprised someone in the shadows:* **MULHOLLAND**.

OLD PROSTITUTE: Anything good on yer mind, Duckie?

*She's blown his cover. **GYPO** gets out of it. **MULHOLLAND** does not know what direction to take to follow **GYPO**; he takes a wrong direction. **OLD PROSTITUTE** cackles a laugh and disappears again. The last word is left to **EVANGELIST**:*

EVANGELIST: At this stage some of you may be thinking that I'm not the jolliest of boys, that I know no joy in life and that I am determined to see no one else does either. That is not so. For when I'm feeling out of sorts through self-denial I whistle, I whistle vigorously, and that, I can tell you, relieves me remarkably, that, I can tell you, lets off some steam.

*Lights changing and **FIGURES** emerging from the darkness. (**MULLIGAN'S VOICE** over if required.) The **FIGURES** appear to be women in various states of undress.*

SCENE EIGHT

*Aunt Betty's Brothel. **AUNT BETTY**: middle-aged to elderly; affects genteel manners which often break down. **MAGGIE** from Tipperary: big boned, red faced, unaffected. **PHYLLIS**: neurotic, English; wears a small hat with a veil which hangs over her face; a short fur coat (?); she keeps at a remove from the others as much as possible. And **CHRISTINA** and **BRIDGET**. The men present are **FARMER** and **STUDENT**. (**OTHERS** as/if the budget allows.) And some dance-tune/song as from a gramophone.*

There's been some knocking at the front door, off, and voices:

PIMP: Who's that?

GYPO: Open up and find out!

PIMP: Yiz can't come in!

GYPO: What's the monkey-trickin' for?

*GYPO comes in, **PIMP** (Bernard) perhaps hanging out of him.*
***GYPO** is pleased at what he sees.*

AUNT BETTY: Good Heavens!

GYPO: God bless all here – save the cat!

AUNT BETTY: What is this?!

STUDENT: Homo pithecanthropus!

AUNT BETTY: Bernard! (*Meaning 'deal with him'*)

PIMP: Private party, friend, on your way.

GYPO: So you're the pimp with yer black-jack in yer pocket –
G'wan outa that! (*He laughs, brushing Pimp aside*)

AUNT BETTY: Pimp? Such language! Bernard is my nephew!
(*Then, rasps:*) What d'yiz want?

GYPO: Such a question, such a question!

AUNT BETTY: Bernard! What is the matter with you! (*'Deal
with him'*)

GYPO: (*Laughs, brushing Pimp aside again:*) G'wan outa that!
I want a drink – an' anythin' else that's goin'.

AUNT BETTY: On your way! –

MAGGIE: Ary, let him stay –

AUNT BETTY: You've lost your way! –

MAGGIE: This dry bunch/pair/party we have here –

GYPO: I've money! –

AUNT BETTY: No-no-no, you're wasting your time, you're...

He has produced his roll of money –

Celebrating?

GYPO: I'm – that's it, mother! – celebratin'. I said to mesel', why shouldn't I, this wan night, a few bob on the women an' a few drinks to keep me supper warm before I... before I... (*He can't remember.*) Me head is swimmin'! (*He slaps a pound into her hand:*) Now, mother!

AUNT BETTY: Aunt. Aunt Betty.

GYPO: Aunt Betty!

AUNT BETTY: Christina, drinks!

GYPO: For the house, Christina!

AUNT BETTY: And, what is your name?

GYPO: That's – that's for you to know and me to find out! (*He laughs*)

AUNT BETTY: (*To the room*) Did yous all hear that?

STUDENT: D'you want me to deal with him, Aunt Betty?

AUNT BETTY: Bernard! (*Aside to* **PIMP**) Apperset the rosenchat. (*Meaning 'Control the Student'*)

Which **PIMP** *effects by backing* **STUDENT** *to a chair and seating him in it.*

(*Continues to* **GYPO**) I don't know what houses you've been in before but – Yes?

GYPO: (*Finger up.*) Never again.

AUNT BETTY: Good, because – yes?

GYPO: Dirty places – Biddy Burke's, Sligo Cissy's an' the rest of them.

AUNT BETTY: Good, because – Are you listening? – before I introduce you to my girls, we have one rule here: no trouble.

GYPO: Aunt Betty.

AUNT BETTY: Because I always keep a kettle of boiling water in there, and if there's trouble that's how I deal with it.

GYPO: Aunt Betty.

CHRISTINA *arrives with a tray of drinks.*

Good on yeh! (*He takes two drinks off the tray.*) Good health!

FARMER: Hey, don't drink the lot!

STUDENT: Savage! Over here, Chrissie! –

FARMER: What are yeh callin' a round for if you're going to drink it all?

GYPO: Divil take ye! Another round, Christina, that's the girl!

FARMER: And a round for the house on me!

GYPO: And another on me!

FARMER: And another on me!

GYPO: And another and another on me!

Applause, laughter, cheers. Music. Trays of drinks, money changing hands.

AUNT BETTY: Assist Christina, girls. You too, Phyllis. God bless the farmer, the backbone of our country! (*Sighs with satisfaction to herself*) Like old times, my dear! (*To* **GYPO**) And those are my girls.

GYPO: I'll never ever again go near them other dirty houses.

AUNT BETTY: Other houses may exceed us in numbers but never in beauty. See Bridget here. Hmm? Are you musical? Sing something, my dear. 'Lift up my finger and I – '

BRIDGET: (*Sings*) 'Some people wear a frown when a thing goes wrong/ Some people swear and cuss, others sing a song/ I don't do either, that's all napoo/ When a thing goes wrong for me, here is what I do:/ I lift up my finger and I say tweet-tweet, shush-shush, now-now, come-come...' (*Or some other song.*)

GYPO: Twish-twish, nush-nush, come-come'!

AUNT BETTY: And Christina: Pert, plump. Hmm? Christina nor Bridget are spoken for yet tonight – These tardy boys!

***FARMER** sweeps **BRIDGET** to himself*

Spoke too soon! – God bless the farmer! And this is Margaret.

MAGGIE: Maggie. How yeh!

GYPO: I'm very pleased to meet yeh, miss. Never ever again! (*Will he go to the other places.*) 'Lisht up my finger an' I say hush-twish, slish-twish, come-come!'

All laughing. Others putting him right in the song. Party spirit.

AUNT BETTY: Gentlemen, ladies! D'yiz want to get me run in be the polis?

GYPO: Shhhh – whist! It's alright, mother, yer a nice girl.

AUNT BETTY: But which of my girls would you like? Make your choice.

GYPO: Well, lemme see... I think I'll take yourself first, mother – for the experience! (*He grabs at her, winking at the others.*)

AUNT BETTY: Heavens, good heavens, heavens! Boys, girls! But what kind of lady d'yiz like?

GYPO: I like – I like – I like a lady with – with good sharp teeth!

They laugh. He laughs with them, but he's highly excited. ***AUNT BETTY** leaves them to it.*

I like – I like – I've been sayin' to meself this while back: before I die I must be in among big beautiful women, soft big beautiful women with – with good sharp teeth! And swally meself in an ocean of drink! Good health!

Now he notices **PHYLLIS**¸ *who is sitting alone; half fur coat, hat and veil.*

To himself) Hah? (*Looks back at the others*) Hah?

CHRISTINA: (*Whispers*) Our English Rose.

GYPO: (*Whispers*) Rose?

CHRISTINA: Miss stuck-up ignorant thing that thinks she's better than what God turned her into.

GYPO: Rose? Aren't yeh hot in the fur coat?

He's circling her, like a dog circling a cat. He reaches in to touch her. She draws herself up in the chair. As he reaches again she hisses, spits at him.

OTHERS: Oooo!

CHRISTINA: (*English accent*) 'You animal!'

PHYLLIS: Yes, swine!

OTHERS: Oooo!

GYPO: I pick her.

PHYLLIS: You're all pigs!

AUNT BETTY: (*Returns*) Now what is this nonsense again, Phyllis? Stop it at once. You know where you'd be only for me. (*She is undressing* **PHYLLIS**.)

CHRISTINA: 'My dahling husband took another woman!' –

AUNT BETTY: We go through this every time and you always give in in the end.

CHRISTINA: 'Then that horrid man did this to me!'

BRIDGET: 'This to me!' –

CHRISTINA: 'This!' –

BRIDGET: 'This!' –

CHRISTINA: 'This!' –

BRIDGET: 'This!' –

PHYLLIS: Yes!

The above from **CHRISTINA** *and* **BRIDGET** *– 'This!' – swivelling their heads to show their faces in profile, culminating with* **PHYLLIS'S** *'Yes!', showing her face in profile, hideously disfigured.*

GYPO *recoils at the sight.*

AUNT BETTY *continues to undress* **PHYLLIS** *until she stands in her slip and bare feet. Whereas earlier* **PHYLLIS'S** *sound was as much laughing as crying, now she's crying softly.*

AUNT BETTY: I'm fed up of your swagger, Phyllis. As long as I keep you here, you're no better – or worse – than anyone else who takes a bite or sup in my house. Count your blessings, my dear. You're very well formed. See! Hmm? In figure and limb.

PHYLLIS: (*Softly*) I'm not a prostitute.

She embraces **AUNT BETTY**. *And as* **AUNT BETTY** *holds her, in a maternal way, she explains to* **GYPO**:

AUNT BETTY: One of our own – a patriot – did this to her when he found out she was an English officer's wife. (*She stands away from Phyllis, as to admire her*) And just as one woman is as good as another, so is one man as good as the next, and you're going with him.

GYPO: (*Apologetically*) No.

PHYLLIS: (*Has not lifted her eyes*) All I want is to go home.

GYPO: Where's your home?

MAGGIE: England.

GYPO: What'll bring yeh home? What'll it cost?

MAGGIE: A few quid.

PHYLLIS: I should never have come here, I should have gone to the police.

GYPO: (*Continues very subdued*) Keep away from that lot. The rascals. Here. (*He's holding out some money to her.*)

AUNT BETTY: What's this?

GYPO: Don't be afraid, take it. 'Tis enough to get yeh home. (*He puts the money in her hand*) Go on now, an' keep away from the police, I'm tellin' yeh.

AUNT BETTY: (*Staying Phyllis*) That's all very well, but she owes me two pounds ten, and who's going to pay me that?

GYPO: Shut yer gob, here's two pounds for yeh an' that's enough!

He sits in a chair, depressed. **PHYLLIS** *slips away.*

CHRISTINA: The poxy English whore!

AUNT BETTY: Christina! Go to your room! At once madam! And you may stay there until I find suitable company for you!

CHRISTINA *goes off, so does* **AUNT BETTY**, *so do* **BRIDGET**, **FARMER**, **STUDENT** *and* **PIMP**. **MAGGIE** *and* **GYPO** *remain.*

Off, a clock chimes one.

MAGGIE: (*Watching him; sings, quietly*) 'Alone, all alone, by the wave-washed shore, all alone in the crowded hall...'

He sighs as in a half-memory of something, then bows his head.

'But I never will forget the sweet maid that I met...'

GYPO: } (*Absently*) 'In the valley of Slievenamon'

MAGGIE: } 'In the valley of Slievenamon'

GYPO: Get me a bottle! Who's comin' to bed with me before the bank is broke?

MAGGIE: I am, Gypo, me bould son o' Gosha!

Lights changing and:

MULLIGAN'S VOICE: I bear no fellow-man a grudge. Yous are the ones with the grudges. The McPhilip family an' ourselves had our troubles but we're not the kind to carry grievances. I bore no grudge again' Frankie McPhilip, the Lord have mercy on his soul. His troubles are over for him now ...

SCENE NINE

GYPO is in bed in Aunt Betty's. MAGGIE has removed his jacket and is removing his boots. That done, she will remove some of her own clothes and get into bed with him. There is a bottle of whiskey and she pours a glass for herself. She's enjoying his undemanding company. He's depressed.

MAGGIE: An' yeh've no girl, Gypo?

GYPO: I haven't.

MAGGIE: Don't be tellin' me lies now.

GYPO: I haven't.

MAGGIE: Well, no doubt, but that's a shame because you're a whale of an ojus great man. An' that's a fact. But fact an' all as it is, I've doubts you'll knock any rights out of this Judy or any other Judy tonight.

GYPO: Maggie, I'm very sad.

MAGGIE: Why is that now?

GYPO: I don't know.

MAGGIE: The Englishwoman, is it?

GYPO: No, the creature. I don't know what came on me there. And you're every bit as fine a woman. Finer.

MAGGIE: (*Chuckles. Then:*) You don't know me?

GYPO: How?

MAGGIE: Now!

GYPO: Hah?

MAGGIE: You're puzzled.

GYPO: I am.

MAGGIE: Will I tell you? Clancy, I'm Maggie Clancy, Tom Clancy's daughter from out the Clonmel Road.

GYPO: Wha'? Tom with the pigs is it wan time?

MAGGIE: Now you have me!

GYPO: Ara stop!

MAGGIE: Now for yeh!

GYPO: Well-well, well-well, is that who I'm with? Tom Clancy's daughter! (*He throws an arm around her.*)

MAGGIE: Go easy now till I finish this! (*The glass of whiskey.*) Sure I used to see yeh goin' the road to Mass of a Sunday. You wouldn't have known me, I was only small then. Or in the bog – didn't ye have a bank of turf next to ours? – with your ass an' cart.

GYPO: We did. Well-well, well-well!

MAGGIE: Now!

GYPO: An' what has yeh up here?

MAGGIE: Oh! Seán, me brother, got married: (*to*) one of the Kennys from Bullaun side, and brought her into the house: and me mother there an' Bina and Winifred and meself and Jimmy.

GYPO: An' Paddy.

MAGGIE: No, Paddy went to England. And the three rooms for the lot of us. Declare to Christ, if I'd stayed on I'd've pulled the head offa that Kenny one.

GYPO: Paddy was nice.

MAGGIE: He was. (*Laughing at herself.*) And a class of notion in me head that I'd meet maybe a Spaniard up here. Now! Wasn't I the simpleton?

GYPO: Sure ye were well-off.

MAGGIE: We were. Wan time. And I was sent to school. And I was a good scholar. (*She laughs again:*) Wait'll I tell yeh! D'you know how much money I made (*on*) me first night at this game? Four pounds. But it was beginner's luck.

GYPO: ... I wish I never left, Maggie. (*He's becoming tearful.*) Spreadin' the turf for me father ... an' bringin' it home ... an', Lord, that ass we had - a mare – an' she was nearly as strong as meself ... (*He's crying:*) An' me mother ... scoldin' me. I wish I could fly out that window now this minute and go home an' see me mother an' father. I miss them.

MAGGIE: Yerra, Gypo, *a stór.*

GYPO: I'm sorry for cryin' in front of yeh, Maggie. But there's something terrible wrong with the world tonight.

MAGGIE: There-there, there-there, sleep Gypo, that's what you need. And won't I be here for you when you wake up? Gimme that shirt of yours and your socks and anything else and I'll be giving them a rinse out for you. Sit up till I get your shirt off.

GYPO: On me solemn oath, I have no girl, Maggie.

MAGGIE: Stop your codology now!

He starts to giggle.

What's on yeh?

GYPO: Yer ticklin' me.

MAGGIE: (*Tickling him*) Ory! Ory!

And she's laughing: he's tickling her. They are rolling in the bed.

The silhouette of figures entering the room: **AUNT BETTY,**

leading **MULHOLLAND** *– perhaps with gun drawn.* **AUNT BETTY** *leaves.*

MAGGIE: (*Whispers*) There's someone in the room.

Silence.

GYPO *gets the paper money he has left and slips it to her.*

What're you doin'? Not at all!

GYPO: Sh-sh-sh! (*Whispers*) Give one of them to Katie Fox: you'll find her up in Biddy Burke's. Hello, Bartley! Time to go, is it?

MULHOLLAND: Yes. We're late.

GYPO: Gimme me boots, Maggie. Court of rein- reinstatement, isn't it?

MULHOLLAND: Yes.

GYPO: Where's me hat?

MULHOLLAND: Hurry up.

GYPO: Who're yeh givin' orders to?

MULHOLLAND: Not my orders. They're waitin' for us.

GYPO: Well, so long, Maggie! 'Twas grand meetin' yeh.

MAGGIE: So long, Gypo!

*He leaves with **MULHOLLAND**.*

*Lights changing. **FIGURES** emerging.*

SCENE TEN

*We are returned to present time, the Court of Inquiry, the room in a basement, the hooded judges, et cetera. A clock is chiming four, off. **GALLAGHER'S** speech in the dark and as the lights come up.*

GALLAGHER: Mr Mulligan's statement has been checked out and corroborated satisfactorily by witnesses, so need he be detained any longer?

1ST JUDGE: You'll be taken home, Mr Mulligan, in the car that brought you here. Your circumstances and the inconvenience caused to you tonight will be brought up at our next Relief Committee meeting. You can go.

GALLAGHER: (*Holds out money to him*) For the present, this might help.

***MULLIGAN** refuses the money. He stops as he's leaving to speak to **MARY**.*

MULLIGAN: Miss, I'm sorry for your trouble.

GALLAGHER: Address the court if you've anything further to say.

MULLIGAN: I'll address who I like! Yeh think yer a great man, Gallagher, but I don't think yer any kind of a man at all – or any of yiz. Takin' the law into yer own hands. (*To **GYPO***) It's not for me to condemn you! (*He leaves*)

GALLAGHER: Alright, Gypo, don't waste our time. What did you mean by telling us that story about seeing Peter Mulligan near the Dunboyne eating-house this evening when we now know he was within a stone's throw of his home at the time?

GYPO: What's that? ... But I'd swear to God 'twas him! I'd know the cut of them shoulders anywhere – even if yeh put me head in a bag ... Well, if it wasn't him it must have been somebody like him ... Commandant, I can't make out nothing clear..

GALLAGHER: Let's do it this way then. Give us an account of your whereabouts from the time Frankie McPhilip left you at the Dunboyne until you were brought here tonight.

GYPO: I can't remember! ... Commandant, I'm all mixed up.

GALLAGHER: Alright. Let's see if I can help you. We'll work backwards. Before you were brought here tonight, you were at a house known as Aunt Betty's. You were in the company of a woman called Maggie Clancy. You had a bottle of whiskey which cost you twenty-two and six. You were seen slipping *something* to Maggie Clancy. Bartley Mulholland had this Maggie Clancy followed: She went to a house known as Biddy Burkes where she offered a pound note to Katie Fox, which caused a row to break out between the two women, which concluded in Maggie Clancy's throwing a further three pounds into Katie Fox's face: A sum of four pounds, which was the *something* you'd slipped to her earlier. Earlier – we're still at Aunt Betty's – you bought three – or was it four? – rounds of drink, which cost you – you were giving tips! Three pounds. This astonishing generosity goes on: *Another* three pounds to an English prostitute called Phyllis Peacock, then a further two to Aunt Betty herself. A millionaire's night out: Thirteen pounds, two and six at Aunt Betty's! Where did this money come from? You 'went through an American sailor at the back of Cassidy's pub on Jerome Street': Is that where you got this sum of money? ... Are you going to answer the question?

GYPO: (*To himself*) An' if I say yes?

GALLAGHER: Are you saying yes?

GYPO: An' if I say no?

GALLAGHER: Are you saying no?

GYPO: (*Forlorn*) Commandant, me head is sore, I'm drunk.

GALLAGHER: (*Dismissing the matter*) In any case, there's no American ship in the docks. Before Aunt Betty's, shortly after eleven o'clock, you treated the population of Marlborough Place to fish and chips. Put the conservative cost to you of a pound on that. Then a pound to the fish-'n'-chip man for a broken window, eight shillings to a Mixer Johnson, a new-found friend, a ten-shilling note to a one-legged man who came along and another to the one-legged man's mother. And before departing your courtiers in Marlborough Place a fistful of coins thrown in the air among them: Say five or six shillings – say five. Which brings your spending in Marlborough Place to three pounds thirteen shillings, which brings your total spending to date to sixteen pounds fifteen and six. What? And just before that, about a quarter past ten, you wouldn't buy a drink for myself, Bartley Mulholland and Tommy Connors, your old comrades, in Ryan's public house – what? – round the corner from Titt Street where Frankie McPhilip died tonight.

GYPO: (*Sighs. Then:*) I'll tell ye all about it so.

GALLAGHER: (*Does not want the confession yet.*) No! Let me continue to retrace your steps for you.

1ST JUDGE: Commandant! (*Calling **GALLAGHER**.*)

*While **GALLAGHER** confers with the judges:*

GYPO: A drink. (*Because his mouth is dry.*)

GALLAGHER: (*To **JUDGES** as he comes away from them*) Yes, all this *is* necessary. (*To **GYPO***) Half nine, quarter to ten, before joining us in Ryan's public house –

GYPO: Commandant, could I –

GALLAGHER: You went to Titt Street –

GYPO: Drink, Commandant –

GALLAGHER: Yes, yes, drink I know – You went to Titt Street, to the home of the McPhilip family –

MARY: He wants a drink of water!

GALLAGHER: Does he? He can't have a drink of water! At the McPhilip house you gave – as best eye-witnesses consider – the sum of about ten shillings in coins to Frankie McPhilip's mother. The total of your spending is now at seventeen pounds five and six.

GYPO: I'll tell yeh.

GALLAGHER: Before that, about half eight, where do we find you? Across the river in the south side, no less – you were joined there by Katie Fox of Biddy Burke's fame – in a public house called Farrellys, where you changed two pound notes. This doesn't mean you spent the full two pounds there but considering that you made your way back to our side of the river again and considering the lavish mood of your evening, it isn't an unfair assumption to make that you stopped at a couple of places en route – Would that be so?

GYPO nods, submissively.

Which, all together, would account for – two pounds? So the total is now nineteen pounds, five and six. By the way, how much have you on you now, Gypo?

GYPO, completely docile, produces a handful of coins.

Eight or nine bob. Say nine. Which added to our nineteen pounds five and six, comes to nineteen pounds, fourteen and six, which leaves us five and six short of the twenty pounds we're aiming at. Any ideas where you might have spent five and six?

GYPO shakes his head, sadly.

Well considering the trail of gold you left behind you, it doesn't much matter, does it?

GYPO shakes his head, sadly agreeing.

And timewise, we've got back to eight thirty. I wish it was as easy to track your movements from then back to the time Frankie left you in the Dunboyne. You do that bit for us.

GYPO: (*Nods. He could be talking to himself*) There was something in me mind. I don't remember what. There's always something in me mind and I don't know right what it is. An' Frankie came in. He was lookin' terrible. I even think he was thinkin' of pluggin' himself. It was in his head anyway. 'Was there a guard on the house?' 'No'. He left. I went to the police station. 'I come to collect the twenty pounds reward for information concernin' Francis Joseph McPhilip', I don't know how I done it. D'ye see what I mean? On me pal. They kept me there: oh, an hour anyway, while, I suppose, they was gone for Frankie. Then they gave me the twenty notes ... An' I wasn't drunk.

The JUDGES confer.

MARY goes to GALLAGHER

GYPO continues seated with his head bowed, looking completely submissive. Perhaps the occasional shake of his head to himself, muttering to himself 'I don't know how I done it'. ('how' means 'why'). It's possible that the sentence of death that is given later goes unregistered by him.

MARY: What are you going to do with him?

GALLAGHER: What do you think?

MARY: No!

GALLAGHER: It's the time-honoured way of dealing with an informer.

MARY: Time-*honoured*?

GALLAGHER: I won't irritate you now by trying to convince you of the rightness of how we do things.

MARY: What? (*Silently perhaps*)

The **JUDGES** *have risen.*

GALLAGHER: Wait out there, I'll take you home in a few minutes.

MARY: (*To the Judges*) He doesn't want to *irritate* me! Have mercy! Frankie McPhilip was my brother. I'm not asking that a life be taken for his. Look at him! (*Meaning 'Look at* **GYPO**') And I know that Frankie wouldn't want this. This is the way to justice and equality in the New Ireland?! For God's sake ...

GALLAGHER *takes her off.*

1ST JUDGE: Gypo Nolan, the court finds you guilty of breaking the binding and irrevocable oath of allegiance and secrecy to the Revolutionary Organisation of Ireland which you swore to uphold, of betraying the trust placed in you and of informing against a brother and bringing about his death. In keeping with the rules this court condemns you to death. The sentence will be carried out in one hour from now in the Wicklow mountains. Comrade Connors, you will be in charge of the execution party. Report to me at headquarters when your mission has been accomplished. The business of the court is now concluded.

The **JUDGES** *are retiring.* **CONNORS**, *confers with* **MULHOLLAND** *and the* **GUARDS** *present.* **GYPO'S** *seeming attitude of submission is disarming. They start to draw lots, talking in whispers, to see who draws the short straw, i.e. matchstick, to decide who is to be the executioner ...*

And **GYPO'S** *frown is deepening; he is shaking his head and sighing to himself; his muttering is growing louder; he is genuinely perplexed and his frustration is mounting.*

GYPO: An' I wasn't drunk, I wasn't drunk. D'yeh see what I mean? But I sold me pal. I don't know how I done it. Can no one tell me how I informed on Frankie? (*He's shouting.*) An' I wasn't drunk! Can no one tell me!

He is not thinking of escape in this moment: But the **GUARDS** *and* **JUDGES** *have been caught unawares: They are turning towards* **GYPO**, *as to close on him, drawing their guns. He throws his head back and bellows like an enraged animal, and goes berserk. He hurtles himself at them. They fall about him as do the chairs, table, and* **GALLAGHER** *too, who is returning with gun drawn. And he runs for it, up the steps and out of the place.* **GALLAGHER** *fires his gun, the bullet hitting/grazing* **GYPO** *as he escapes.*

GUARDS *in pursuit. Great activity inside and outside. More shots discharged outside. A car starting up, a truck/van starting up, engines revving, running feet.* **VOICES***:*

> Cover the Bridges!
>
> He'll try to go south!
>
> Who fired the shots out here?
>
> Me!
>
> Did you hit him?
>
> I couldn't tell!
>
> What direction did he take?
>
> Beaver Street!

Beaver Street, up towards Mount William Road!...

Voices, running feet, engines fading, during which **MARY** *comes in. She sees* **GYPO'S** *hat on the floor and she picks it up and just looks at it.*

SCENE ELEVEN

Katie's and Louisa's room and the landing outside the door. **KATIE** *and* **LOUISA** *are high on drugs.* **KATIE** *by turn, is laughing and crying,* **LOUISA** *cackles in complement and offers comfort. The statue of St. Joseph has been reinstated as a beloved member of the household.*

KATIE: I don't give a damn!

LOUISA: (*Tells the statue*) She doesn't give a damn!

KATIE: So there! (*She laughs. And now she's crying.*) Wasn't I the fool to answer them questions for them!

LOUISA: (*To the statue*) Wasn't she the fool?

KATIE: Yaa, Pugnose! (*Laughing. Now serious.*) D'yiz think they'll croak him? (*Crying.*) Me man, Gypo. They've croaked him already sure.

LOUISA: Oh they have, they have. But there-there, there-there. No man is worth it, except maybe me own little St J, an' he's not like an ordinary man at all 'cause he's blesséd.

KATIE: Did yiz know me grandfather was Duke of Clonliffey?

LOUISA: (*To statue*) Listen to every word she's sayin', darlin'.

KATIE: An' me mother had royalty on her father's side.

LOUISA: King o' Spain –

KATIE: An' not to the King of England either, but related to me bould King o' Spain.

LOUISA: Oranges, oranges.

KATIE: Where they grow oranges plentiful as potatoes.

LOUISA: Shannon, the Shannon.

KATIE: An' where wine flows free as the waters of the Shannon.

LOUISA: (*The statue has swiveled in her hands so that it is facing the door. Whispers:*) There's someone there!

KATIE: And I was born in a palace, big as the County of Waterford.

*And indeed, there is someone outside (what is meant to be) the door. **GYPO**. He has arrived during the above and hangs there, hurt, bleeding, afraid to knock.*

LOUISA: (*Whispering*) There's someone there.

KATIE: Is there someone there?

LOUISA: Who's there, at wanct (*once*) ?!

GYPO: Katie, Katie, let me in.

LOUISA: It's his ghost.

KATIE: (*Frightened*) Who's that?

GYPO: It's only me, Katie.

LOUISA: Don't let him in.

GYPO: I'm hit. I escaped out of the Bogey Hole. They're after me, they're goin' to plug me. Katie, darlin', open the door.

LOUISA: Bolt it – double bolt it.

KATIE is hesitant over what to do.

GYPO: The bridges are covered. Just to lie down quiet for a few hours till I can make me way south tomorrow.

LOUISA: Maggie, Maggie.

*Which cue decides the matter for **KATIE** and she 'double-bolts' the door.*

KATIE: Why don't yiz go to Maggie, Maggie, Maggie! Maggie Clancy, yaa, that big Tipperary heifer! Yaa, I know yiz now! Pug nose!

GYPO: Shhh, shhh, they'll hear yeh!

KATIE: Pug nose! I wasn't good enough for yiz!

GYPO: Shh, shh! I gave her a quid for yeh.

KATIE: An' three to her!

LOUISA: (*Statue has swivelled in her hands so that it is facing the street*) They're in the street.

KATIE: Yaa, yaa!

GYPO: For the love o' God, Katie, whist, they'll hear yeh!

*And, indeed, a car, and perhaps a van can be heard coming down the street; now they are passing the house. And now **LOUISA** cues:*

LOUISA: Inform, inform.

KATIE: (*Calls out to the street:*) He's here, he's here, Gypo Nolan the informer is here!

*Outside, in the street, the van and the car reversing and coming to a stop. Footsteps in the street. **VOICES**:*

Number 61:

Cover the back door!

You take the front!

Cover the top of the street! ...

GYPO feels the top of his head for his hat to find it is not there. He knows the game is up. He straightens himself, preparatory to going out to the street.

KATIE: (*Now weeping, regrets what she has done*) Gypo?

GYPO: So long, Katie! (*He leaves.*)

KATIE: D'yous know what I'm goin' to tell yiz, Louisa? This is a quare aul world, but when I'm dead I'm goin' to have a holy well built to me out on the Malahide Road and there'll be a spell on it, an' anyone I don't like'll get up thirsty in the middle of the night an'll walk barefoot to it to drink three cupful o' the holy water, not knowin' I'll have it poisoned.

Outside, three shots ring out.

SCENE TWELVE

Street. (The street is near a church. The 'dead' bell, as for mass for the dead, is ringing.) **GYPO** *totters in the middle of the street, but he is still managing to keep upright.* **CONNORS,** **MULHOLLAND** *and a* **GUARD,** *with guns drawn, and* **GALLAGHER** *form a wide circle around him; then, as they retreat off,* **GALLAGHER** *produces his gun and shoots* **GYPO.**

GYPO *sinks to his knees.*

The McPhilip family – **MOTHER, FATHER, MARY** *– (And optionally,* **UNCLE MICK***) come along, on their way to Mass.* **MOTHER** *goes to* **GYPO.**

MOTHER: Aw, Gypo, me poor son, what have they done to yiz?

GYPO: I informed on Frankie, Mrs McPhilip. Forgive me.

MOTHER: I forgive yeh, Gypo. Yous didn't know what yiz were doin'.

She is kneeling beside him, cradling his head in her lap.

Leabharlanna Poiblí Chathair Bhaile Átha Cliath
Dublin City Public Libraries

CARYSFORT PRESS

The Press aims to produce high quality publications which, though written and/or edited by academics, will be made accessible to a general readership. The organisation would also like to provide a forum for critical thinking in the Arts in Ireland, again keeping the needs and interests of the general public in view.

The company publishes contemporary Irish writing for and about the theatre.

Editorial and publishing inquiries to:

CARYSFORT PRESS Ltd

58 Woodfield, Scholarstown Road,
Rathfarnham, Dublin 16,
Republic of Ireland

T (353 1) 493 7383 F (353 1) 406 9815
e: info@carysfortpress.com
www.carysfortpress.com

Carysfort Press was formed in the summer of 1998. It receives annual funding from the Arts Council.

The directors believe that drama is playing an ever-increasing role in today's society and that enjoyment of the theatre, both professional and amateur, currently plays a central part in Irish culture.

NEW TITLES

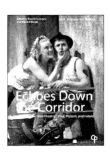

ECHOES DOWN THE CORRIDOR: IRISH THEATRE – PAST, PRESENT, AND FUTURE

EDITED BY PATRICK LONERGAN AND RIANA O'DWYER

This collection of fourteen new essays explores Irish theatre from exciting new perspectives. How has Irish theatre been received internationally - and, as the country becomes more multicultural, how will international theatre influence the development of drama in Ireland? These and many other important questions.

ISBN   978-1-904505-25-9
€20

GOETHE AND ANNA AMALIA: A FORBIDDEN LOVE?

BY ETTORE GHIBELLINO, TRANS. DAN FARRELLY

In this study Ghibellino sets out to show that the platonic relationship between Goethe and Charlotte von Stein – lady-in-waiting to Anna Amalia, the Dowager Duchess of Weimar – was used as part of a cover-up for Goethe's intense and prolonged love relationship with the Duchess Anna Amalia herself. The book attempts to uncover a hitherto closely-kept state secret. Readers convinced by the evidence supporting Ghibellino's hypothesis will see in it one of the very great love stories in European history – to rank with that of Dante and Beatrice, and Petrarch and Laura.

ISBN   978-1-904505-24-2
EAN   9781904505242
€25

MODERN DEATH: THE END OF HUMANITY

TRANS: DAN FARRELLY

Modern Death is written in the form of a symposium, in which a government agency brings together a group of experts to discuss a strategy for dealing with an ageing population. The speakers take up the thread of the ongoing debates about care for the aged and about euthanasia. In dark satirical mode the author shows what grim developments are possible.

ISBN 978-1-904505-28-0
€8

SHIFTING SCENES:
IRISH THEATRE-GOING 1955-1985

NICHOLAS GRENE AND CHRIS MORASH

Transcript of conversations with John Devitt, academic and reviewer, about his lifelong passion for the theatre. A fascinating and entertaining insight into Dublin theatre over the course of thirty years provided by Devitt's vivid reminiscences and astute observations.

ISBN 978-1-904505-33-4
€10

IRISH THEATRE IN ENGLAND,
IRISH THEATRICAL DIASPORA SERIES: 2

EDITED BY RICHARD CAVE AND BEN LEVITAS

Irish theatre in England has frequently illustrated the complex relations between two distinct cultures. How English reviewers and audiences interpret Irish plays is often decidedly different from how the plays were read in performance in Ireland. How certain Irish performers have chosen to be understood in Dublin is not necessarily how audiences in London have perceived their constructed stage personae. Though a collection by diverse authors, the twelve essays in this volume investigate these issues from a variety of perspectives that together chart the trajectory of Irish performance in England from the mid-nineteenth century till today.

ISBN 978-1-904505-26-6
€20

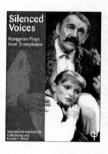

SILENCED VOICES
HUNGARIAN PLAYS FROM TRANSYLVANIA

SELECTED AND TRANSLATED BY
CSILLA BERTHA AND DONALD E. MORSE

The five plays are wonderfully theatrical, moving fluidly from absurdism to tragedy, and from satire t the darkly comic. Donald Morse and Csilla Bertha's translations capture these qualities perfectly, giving voice to the 'forgotten playwrights of Central Europe'. They also deeply enrich our understanding of the relationship between art, ethics, and politics Europe.

ISBN 978-1-904505-34-1
€25

EDNA O'BRIEN
'NEW CRITICAL PERSPECTIVES'
EDITED BY KATHRYN LAING
SINÉAD MOONEY AND MAUREEN O'CONNOR

The essays collected here illustrate some of the range, complexity, and interest of Edna O'Brien as a fiction writer and dramatist…They will contribute to a broader appreciation of her work and to an evolution of new critical approaches, as well as igniting more interest   in the many unexplored areas of her considerable oeuvre.

ISBN 1-904505-20-1
€20

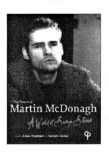

THE THEATRE OF MARTIN MCDONAGH
'A WORLD OF SAVAGE STORIES'
EDITED BY LILIAN CHAMBERS AND
EAMONN JORDAN

The book is a vital response to the many challenges set by McDonagh for those involved in the production and reception of his work. Critics and commentators from around the world offer a diverse range of often provocative approaches. What is not surprising is the focus and commitment of the engagement, given the controversial and stimulating nature of the work.

ISBN 1-904505-19-8
€35

IRELAND ON STAGE:
BECKETT AND AFTER
EDITORS: HIROKO MIKAMI, MINAKO
OKAMURO, NAOKO YAGI

A collection of ten essays on contemporary Irish theatre. The focus is primarily on Irish playwrights and their works, both in text and on the stage, in the latter half of the twentieth century. The essays range from Samuel Beckett to Brian Friel, Frank McGuinness, Marina Carr, and Conor McPherson. There is frequent reference back to Wilde, Yeats, Synge, Shaw, O'Casey, and Joyce.

ISBN   978-1-904505-23-5
€20

BRIAN FRIEL'S DRAMATIC ARTISTRY
'THE WORK HAS VALUE'
EDITED BY DONALD E. MORSE, CSILLA
BERTHA, AND MÁRIA KURDI

Brian Friel's Dramatic Artistry presents a refreshingly broad range of voices: new work from some of the leading English-speaking authorities on Friel, and fascinating essays from scholars in Germany, Italy, Portugal, and Hungary. This book will deepen our knowledge and enjoyment of Friel's work.

ISBN 1-904505-17-1
€25

OUT OF HISTORY
'ESSAYS ON THE WRITINGS OF SEBASTIAN BARRY'

EDITED WITH AN INTRODUCTION BY CHRISTINA HUNT MAHONY

The essays address Barry's engagement with the contemporary cultural debate in Ireland and also with issues that inform postcolonial criticial theory. The range and selection of contributors has ensured a high level of critical expression and an insightful assessment of Barry and his works.

ISBN 1-904505-18-X
€20

IRISH THEATRE ON TOUR
IRISH THEATRICAL DIASPORA SERIES: 1

EDITED BY NICHOLAS GRENE AND CHRIS MORASH

'Touring has been at the strategic heart of Druid's artistic policy since the early eighties. Everyone has the right to see professional theatre in their own communities. Irish theatre on tour is a crucial part of Irish theatre as a whole'. *Garry Hynes*

ISBN 1-904505-13-9
€20

GEORGE FITZMAURICE:
'WILD IN HIS OWN WAY'

BIOGRAPHY OF AN ABBEY PLAYWRIGHT
BY FIONA BRENNAN
WITH A FOREWORD BY FINTAN O'TOOLE

Fiona Brennan's...introduction to his considerable output allows us a much greater appreciation and understanding of Fitzmaurice, the one remaining under-celebrated genius of twentieth-century Irish drama.
Conall Morrison

ISBN 1-904505-16-3
€20

IRISH LITERATURE FEMINIST PERSPECTIVES
IASIL STUDIES IN IRISH WRITING

EDITED BY PATRICIA COUGHLAN AND TINA O'TOOLE

The collection discusses texts from the early 18th century to the present. A central theme of the book is the need to renegotiate the relations of feminism with nationalism and to transact the potential contest of these two important narratives, each possessing powerful emancipatory force. *Irish Literature: Feminist Perspectives* contributes incisively to contemporary debates about Irish culture, gender and ideology.

ISBN 978-1-904505-35-8
€20

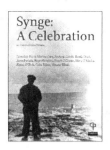

EAST OF EDEN
NEW ROMANIAN PLAYS
EDITED BY ANDREI MARINESCU

Four of the most promising Romanian playwrights, young and very young, are in this collection, each one with a specific way of seeing the Romanian reality, each one with a style of communicating an articulated artistic vision of the society we are living in.
Ion Caramitru, General Director Romanian National Theatre Bucharest

ISBN 1-904505-15-5
€10

SYNGE: A CELEBRATION
EDITED BY COLM TÓIBÍN

A collection of essays by some of Ireland's most creative writers on the work of John Millington Synge, featuring Sebastian Barry , Marina Carr, Anthony Cronin, Roddy Doyle, Anne Enright, Hugo Hamilton, Joseph O'Connor, Mary O'Malley, Fintan O'Toole, Colm Toibin, Vincent Woods.

ISBN 1-904505-14-7
€15 Paperback

POEMS 2000–2005
BY HUGH MAXTON

Poems 2000-2005 is a transitional collection written while the author – also known to be W. J. Mc Cormack, literary historian – was in the process of moving back from London to settle in rural Ireland.

ISBN 1-904505-12-0
€10

HAMLET
THE SHAKESPEAREAN DIRECTOR
BY MIKE WILCOCK

"This study of the Shakespearean director as viewed through various interpretations of HAMLET is a welcome addition to our understanding of how essential it is for a director to have a clear vision of a great play. It is an important study from which all of us who love Shakespeare and who understand the importance of continuing contemporary exploration may gain new insights."

From the Foreword, by Joe Dowling, Artistic Director, The Guthrie Theater, Minneapolis, MN

ISBN 1-904505-00-7
€20

GEORG BÜCHNER: WOYZECK
A NEW TRANSLATION BY DAN FARRELLY

The most up-to-date German scholarship of
Thomas Michael Mayer and Burghard
Dedner has finally made it possible to establish
an authentic sequence of scenes. The wide-
spread view that this play is a prime example of
loose, open theatre is no longer sustainable.
Directors and teachers are challenged to "read
it again".

ISBN 1-904505-02-3
€10

MUSICS OF BELONGING:
THE POETRY OF MICHEAL O'SIADHAIL
EDITED BY MARC CABALL AND DAVID F. FORD

An overall account is given of O'Siadhail's life, his
work and the reception of his poetry so far. There
are close readings of some poems, analyses of his
artistry in matching diverse content with both
classical and innovative forms, and studies of
recurrent themes such as love, death, language,
music, and the shifts of modern life.

Paperback €25
ISBN 978-1-904505-22-8

Casebound €50
ISBN: 978-1-904505-21-1

CRITICAL MOMENTS
FINTAN O'TOOLE ON MODERN IRISH THEATRE
EDITED BY JULIA FURAY & REDMOND O'HANLON

This new book on the work of Fintan O'Toole,
the internationally acclaimed theatre critic and
cultural commentator, offers percussive analyses
and assessments of the major plays and
playwrights in the canon of modern Irish
theatre. Fearless and provocative in his
judgements, O'Toole is essential reading for
anyone interested in criticism or in the current
state of Irish theatre.

ISBN 1-904505-03-1
€20

THE THEATRE OF MARINA CARR
"BEFORE RULES WAS MADE" - EDITED BY
ANNA MCMULLAN & CATHY LEENEY

As the first published collection of articles on
the theatre of Marina Carr, this volume explores
the world of Carr's theatrical imagination, the
place of her plays in contemporary theatre in
Ireland and abroad and the significance of her
highly individual voice.

ISBN 0-9534-2577-0
€20

THEATRE TALK

VOICES OF IRISH THEATRE PRACTITIONERS
EDITED BY LILIAN CHAMBERS &
GER FITZGIBBON

"This book is the right approach - asking
practitioners what they feel."
Sebastian Barry, Playwright

"... an invaluable and informative collection of
interviews with those who make and shape the
landscape of Irish Theatre."
Ben Barnes, Artistic Director of the Abbey Theatre

ISBN 0-9534-2576-2
€20

SACRED PLAY

SOUL JOURNEYS IN CONTEMPORARY
IRISH THEATRE BY ANNE F. O'REILLY

'Theatre as a space or container for sacred play
allows audiences to glimpse mystery and to
experience transformation. This book charts how
Irish playwrights negotiate the labyrinth of the
Irish soul and shows how their plays contribute
to a poetics of Irish culture that enables a new
imagining. Playwrights discussed are:
McGuinness, Murphy, Friel, Le Marquand Hartigan,
Burke Brogan, Harding, Meehan, Carr, Parker,
Devlin, and Barry.'

ISBN 1-904505-07-4
€25

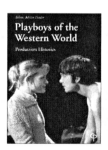

THEATRE OF SOUND

RADIO AND THE DRAMATIC IMAGINATION
BY DERMOT RATTIGAN

An innovative study of the challenges that radio
drama poses to the creative imagination of the
writer, the production team, and the listener.

"A remarkably fine study of radio drama –
everywhere informed by the writer's
professional experience of such drama in the
making…A new theoretical and analytical
approach – informative, illuminating and at all
times readable." *Richard Allen Cave*

ISBN 0-9534-2575-4
€20

PLAYBOYS OF THE WESTERN WORLD

PRODUCTION HISTORIES
EDITED BY ADRIAN FRAZIER

'Playboys of the Western World is a model of
contemporary performance studies.'

'The book is remarkably well-focused: half is a series
of production histories of Playboy performances
through the twentieth century in the UK, Northern
Ireland, the USA, and Ireland. The remainder focuses
on one contemporary performance, that of Druid
Theatre, as directed by Garry Hynes. The various
contemporary social issues that are addressed in
relation to Synge's play and this performance of it
give the volume an additional interest: it shows
how the arts matter.' *Kevin Barry*

ISBN 1-904505-06-6
€20

THE THEATRE OF FRANK MCGUINNESS
STAGES OF MUTABILITY
EDITED BY HELEN LOJEK

The first edited collection of essays about
internationally renowned Irish playwright Frank
McGuinness focuses on both performance and
text. Interpreters come to diverse conclusions,
creating a vigorous dialogue that enriches
understanding and reflects a strong consensus
about the value of McGuinness's complex work.

ISBN 1-904505-01-5
€20

THE DRUNKARD
TOM MURPHY

'The Drunkard is a wonderfully eloquent play.
Murphy's ear is finely attuned to the glories and
absurdities of melodramatic exclamation, and
even while he is wringing out its ludicrous
overstatement, he is also making it sing.'
The Irish Times

ISBN 1-904505-09-0
€10

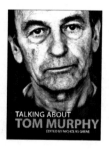

TALKING ABOUT TOM MURPHY
EDITED BY NICHOLAS GRENE

Talking About Tom Murphy is shaped around the
six plays in the landmark Abbey Theatre Murphy
Season of 2001, assembling some of the best-
known commentators on his work: Fintan
O'Toole, Chris Morash, Lionel Pilkington,
Alexandra Poulain, Shaun Richards, Nicholas
Grene and Declan Kiberd.

ISBN 0-9534-2579-7
€15

THE POWER OF LAUGHTER
EDITED BY ERIC WEITZ

The collection draws on a wide range of
perspectives and voices including critics,
playwrights, directors and performers. The result is
a series of fascinating and provocative debates
about the myriad functions of comedy in
contemporary Irish theatre. *Anna McMullan*

As Stan Laurel said, it takes only an onion to cry.
Peel it and weep. Comedy is harder. These essays
listen to the power of laughter. They hear the
tough heart of Irish theatre – hard and wicked
and funny. *Frank McGuinness*

ISBN 1-904505-05-8
€20

THREE CONGREGATIONAL MASSES

BY SEÓIRSE BODLEY,
EDITED BY LORRAINE BYRNE

'From the simpler congregational settings in the Mass of Peace and the Mass of Joy to the richer textures of the Mass of Glory, they are immediately attractive and accessible, and with a distinctively Irish melodic quality.' *Barra Boydell*

ISBN 1-904505-11-2
€15

THE IRISH HARP BOOK

BY SHEILA LARCHET CUTHBERT

This is a facsimile of the edition originally published by Mercier Press in 1993. There is a new preface by Sheila Larchet Cuthbert, and the biographical material has been updated. It is a collection of studies and exercises for the use of teachers and pupils of the Irish harp.

ISBN 1-904505-08-2
€35

GOETHE AND SCHUBERT

ACROSS THE DIVIDE
EDITED BY LORRAINE BYRNE & DAN FARRELLY

Proceedings of the International Conference, 'Goethe and Schubert in Perspective and Performance', Trinity College Dublin, 2003. This volume includes essays by leading scholars – Barkhoff, Boyle, Byrne, Canisius, Dürr, Fischer, Hill, Kramer, Lamport, Lund, Meikle, Newbould, Norman McKay, White, Whitton, Wright, Youens – on Goethe's musicality and his relationship to Schubert; Schubert's contribution to sacred music and the Lied and his setting of Goethe's Singspiel, Claudine. A companion volume of this Singspiel (with piano reduction and English translation) is also available.

ISBN 1-904505-04-X
Goethe and Schubert: Across the Divide. €25

ISBN 0-9544290-0-1
Goethe and Schubert: 'Claudine von Villa Bella'. €14

GOETHE: MUSICAL POET, MUSICAL CATALYST

EDITED BY LORRAINE BYRNE

'Goethe was interested in, and acutely aware of, the place of music in human experience generally - and of its particular role in modern culture. Moreover, his own literary work - especially the poetry and Faust - inspired some of the major composers of the European tradition to produce some of their finest works.' *Martin Swales*

ISBN 1-904505-10-4
€30

GOETHE AND SCHUBERT 'CLAUDINE VON VILLA BELLA'

EDITED BY LORRAINE BYRNE & DAN FARRELLY

Goethe's Singspiel in three acts was set to music by Schubert in 1815. Only Act One of Schuberts's Claudine score is extant. The present volume makes Act One available for performance in English and German. It comprises both a piano reduction by Lorraine Byrne of the original Schubert orchestral score and a bilingual text translated for the modern stage by Dan Farrelly. This is a tale, wittily told, of lovers and vagabonds, romance, reconciliation, and resolution of family conflict.

ISBN 0-9544290-0-1
€14

PROSERPINA: GOETHE'S MELDODRAMA WITH MUSIC BY CARL EBERWEIN, ORCHESTRAL SCORE AND PIANO REDUCTION

EDITOR: LORRAINE BYRNE BODLEY; PREFACE BY NICHOLAS BOYLE

This score, the first edition of Eberwein's setting of Goethe's melodrama, Proserpina, offers an unprecedented examination of Goethe's text and overturns the accepted image of the artist as unmusical. Carl Eberwein's dramatic setting of Goethe's melodrama, Proserpina, for solo voice (speaking part) and orchestra, with a choral finale, is highly dramatic in impact and beautifully orchestrated.

ISBN HB: 9781904505273; PB: 9781904505297
€28

A HAZARDOUS MELODY OF BEING: SEOIRSE BODLEY'S SONG CYCLES ON THE POEMS OF MICHEAL O'SIADHAIL

EDITED AND WITH AN INTRODUCTION BY LORRAINE BYRNE BODLEY

This apograph is the first publication of Bodley's O'Siadhail song cycles and is the first book to explore the composer's lyrical modernity from a number of perspectives. Lorraine Byrne Bodley's insightful introduction describes in detail the development and essence of Bodley's musical thinking, the European influences he absorbed which linger in these cycles, and the importance of his work as a composer of the Irish art song.

ISBN 978-1-904505-31-0 (paperback)
€25

THEATRE STUFF (REPRINT)

CRITICAL ESSAYS ON
CONTEMPORARY IRISH THEATRE
EDITED BY EAMONN JORDAN

Best selling essays on the successes and
debates of contemporary Irish theatre at home
and abroad.

Contributors include: Thomas Kilroy, Declan
Hughes, Anna McMullan, Declan Kiberd, Deirdre
Mulrooney, Fintan O'Toole, Christopher Murray,
Caoimhe McAvinchey and Terry Eagleton.

ISBN 0-9534-2571-1
€20

URFAUST

A NEW VERSION OF GOETHE'S
EARLY "FAUST" IN BRECHTIAN MODE
BY DAN FARRELLY

This version is based on Brecht's irreverent and
daring re-interpretation of the German classic.

"Urfaust is a kind of well-spring for German
theatre… The love-story is the most daring and
the most profound in German dramatic
literature." *Brecht*

ISBN 0-9534257-0-3
€10

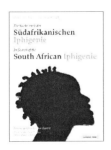

IN SEARCH OF THE
SOUTH AFRICAN IPHIGENIE

BY ERIKA VON WIETERSHEIM
AND DAN FARRELLY

Discussions of Goethe's "Iphigenie auf Tauris"
(Under the Curse) as relevant to women's issues
in modern South Africa: women in family and
public life; the force of women's spirituality;
experience of personal relationships; attitudes to
parents and ancestors; involvement with religion.

ISBN 0-9534-2578-9
€10

THE STARVING
AND OCTOBER SONG

TWO CONTEMPORARY IRISH PLAYS
BY ANDREW HINDS

The Starving, set during and after the siege of
Derry in 1689, is a moving and engrossing
drama of the emotional journey of two men.

October Song, a superbly written family drama
set in real time in pre-ceasefire Derry.

ISBN 0-9534-2574-6
€10

SEEN AND HEARD (REPRINT)

SIX NEW PLAYS BY IRISH WOMEN
EDITED WITH AN INTRODUCTION
BY CATHY LEENEY

A rich and funny, moving and theatrically exciting collection of plays by Mary Elizabeth Burke-Kennedy, Síofra Campbell, Emma Donoghue, Anne Le Marquand Hartigan, Michelle Read and Dolores Walshe.

ISBN 0-9534-2573-8
€20

UNDER THE CURSE

GOETHE'S "IPHIGENIE AUF TAURIS",
IN A NEW VERSION BY DAN FARRELLY

The Greek myth of Iphigenie grappling with the curse on the house of Atreus is brought vividly to life. This version is currently being used in Johannesburg to explore problems of ancestry, religion, and Black African women's spirituality.

ISBN 0-9534-2572-X
€10

HOW TO ORDER
TRADE ORDERS DIRECTLY TO

CMD
Columba Mercier Distribution,
55A Spruce Avenue,
Stillorgan Industrial Park,
Blackrock,
Co. Dublin

T: (353 1) 294 2560
F: (353 1) 294 2564
E: cmd@columba.ie

FOR SALES IN NORTH AMERICA AND CANADA

Dufour Editions Inc.,
124 Byers Road,
PO Box 7,
Chester Springs, PA 19425,
USA

T: 1-610-458-5005
F: 1-610-458-7103